Power Food

Pure recipes by

RENS KROES

For a happy and healthy lifestyle

FAIR WINDS

Copyright

Quarto is the authority on a wide range of topics.

Quarto educates, entertains and enriches the lives of our readers—enthusiasts and lovers of hands-on living.

www.QuartoKnows.com

Text © 2014 Rens Kroes
English translation © 2017 Quarto Publishing Group USA Inc.

First published in the United States of America in 2017 by
Fair Winds Press, an imprint of
Quarto Publishing Group USA Inc.
100 Cummings Center
Suite 406-L
Beverly, Massachusetts 01915-6101
Telephone: (978) 282-9590
Fax: (978) 283-2742
QuartoKnows.com
Visit our blogs at QuartoKnows.com

20 19 18 17   1 2 3 4 5

ISBN: 978-1-59233-744-6

Library of Congress Cataloging-in-Publication Data available

Design and Layout: Bülent Yüksel, www.bybulent.com
Photography: Anne Timmer
Styling: Renske van der Ploeg
Makeup: Yokaw@Angelique Hoorn (cover and inside pages)
Post-production: Neda Gueorguieva
Photography for Recipes and Spreads: Lieke Heijn and Pim Janswaard (Cameron Studio)
Styling for Recipes and Spreads: Lieke Heijn (Cameron Studio)
Culinary Development: Yvonne Jimmink and Jacquline Pietrowski

Printed in China

The information in this book is for educational purposes only. It is not intended to replace the advice of a physician or medical practitioner. Please see your health-care provider before beginning any new health program.

With thanks to

Filippa K. Amsterdam, Raak Amsterdam, Blackbird Coffee, Kimm Bakkers, Yvonne Brok, Bas Jonker, Piet Jonker, Historische Bouwmaterialen in Bambrugge, Stef Kroon and Gijs Stork, Tanja Terstappen, and Stella Willing.

Contents

*I*t's not really a surprise that I'm interested in good and pure food. It's all I know. We were *the* organic family from Eastermar, a small village in Friesland. My *pake* (grandfather) was the village's first organic farmer, my *beppe* (grandmother) was an herbalist, and my mother is a nutritionist. Healthy eating is simply something I grew up with.

When I turned nineteen, I left Friesland for New York. Oh my! That was the time of my life. I put on my high heels and went to the coolest parties, dancing the night away with celebs. By day, I was a student and was conscious of nutrition and its impact on my body. In that regard, New York is paradise and never ceases to inspire me. The raw-food movement was popular there at that time, and I discovered new restaurants (and new dishes) every day, and did my grocery shopping at organic stores. When I went to class, I brought containers of homemade salad, nuts, and fresh smoothies with me. I was stereotypically Dutch, even in New York! People looked at me a bit funny in the beginning, but soon enough my friends started following suit. After a wonderful year in the Big Apple, I moved back to the Netherlands, to Amsterdam. There, I started working at an obesity clinic. That's where I got in touch with the psychological side of eating and it was when I knew I wanted to help people establish healthy eating habits and maintain a healthy lifestyle.

I believe that the combination of healthy eating, enough physical activity, *and* relaxation ensures both fitness and happiness. I call it the holy trinity. You can't achieve happiness in your life by crash dieting, but you *can* by eating good, healthy food, taking care of yourself, and—most of all—deriving enjoyment from doing so. I am a proponent of organic food because it has not been treated with pesticides and it is unprocessed. Not only does organic food just taste better, but also your body is not forced to process unnecessary toxins after eating it. In addition to eating well and exercising, I'm convinced that relaxation is essential. Be good to your body, but also be sure to treat yourself to a relaxing evening with a good movie, a dinner with friends, or a night of dancing. It's at those times that I take a deep breath, smile, and appreciate just how great my life is. *That* is the ultimate form of relaxation for me.

Okay. Ready for action? Is it more work to cook healthy food? Yes, fair is fair. Of course it does take more time to prepare healthy food than to warm up a premade meal in the microwave. But precisely because you prepare your food more mindfully, you appreciate it more. Keep in mind that it might take a little while to get accustomed to your new lifestyle. That's okay. If you make these changes out of love for yourself and your body, after a while, you'll notice that they make you feel better. Whatever you do, don't succumb to stress if things don't work out on day one. Give yourself the time to get into the right flow. I always say that it can take about three months to get there. After that, your mind and body will have adapted to your new habits. Then it's okay if you fall off the wagon every now and then. It happens to me too. I love to go out—preferably enjoying a glass of Champagne (or two) and snacking on some late-night fries on the way home. Healthy? Not really. But a night like that produces instant happiness, and that in itself is so important. It really is fine to enjoy things that are slightly less than healthy from time to time. You'll feel the effects of this on your body and will probably want to get back to your healthy lifestyle as soon as possible afterward.

In putting this book together, I spent hours and hours in the kitchen, tasting, adjusting, and testing the recipes. The finished product is a compilation of my very favorites, from smoothies to go, happiness-inducing breakfasts, simple salads, and pastas, to healthy versions of sinful sweets. I'll also tell you about the effects different vegetables, superfoods, and other ingredients have on your body.

Take the time to enjoy cooking, be kind to yourself, and, above all, enjoy!

Introduction

Rens Kroes

Breakfast

Kick-start your day!

Good morning! I start every day with a glass of warm water and freshly squeezed lemon juice. Because I like to keep my teeth healthy, I drink it with a straw. What a tasty pick-me-up! This kick-start drink has a cleansing effect on the body and gives an instant energy boost. After taking this moment for myself, I make my breakfast, and start my day.

BREAKFAST MUFFINS

DON'T BE FOOLED BY THEIR *sweetness:* THESE MUFFINS PACK A SERIOUS *power breakfast* PUNCH. I USUALLY MAKE ABOUT TEN OF THESE AT A TIME SO I CAN EAT THEM AS A SNACK OR *take them with me* FOR BREAKFAST DURING THE WEEK. WHEN I DO TAKE ONE TO GO, I'LL PICK UP A TASTY COFFEE ON MY WAY TO ENJOY WITH IT. HAPPINESS! THIS RECIPE CALLS FOR *mulberries,* BUT YOU COULD JUST AS EASILY USE APPLE CHUNKS, BLUEBERRIES, OR EVEN *jam,* IF YOU PREFER. THESE MUFFINS ARE ALSO A TASTY, *fun,* NUTRITIOUS BREAKFAST FOR *kids.*

PREPARATION
35 MINUTES

INGREDIENTS
- 1¼ CUPS (100 G) WHOLE OATS
- 1 TEASPOON BAKING POWDER
- 2 RIPE BANANAS
- 3 EGGS
- 2 TEASPOONS GROUND CINNAMON
- 2 TEASPOONS PURE VANILLA EXTRACT
- PINCH OF SALT
- ⅔ CUP (100 G) DRIED BLACK MULBERRIES

SUPPLIES
MUFFIN TIN, MUFFIN LINERS, BLENDER

DIRECTIONS
Preheat the oven to 350°F (180°C). Place liners in 10 cups of a muffin tin.

Combine all the ingredients, except the mulberries, in the blender and process until smooth. Pour the mixture into a bowl and add the mulberries. Stir well. Spoon 2 tablespoons (30 g) of the mixture into each of the lined muffin cups. Bake for 30 minutes. Have a look at them every now and then to make sure they don't brown too much or too quickly.

YIELD: 10 MUFFINS

GRANOLA

MAKE YOUR OWN GRANOLA. IT'S SO MUCH *healthier* WHEN YOU DO! I SPRINKLE MINE ON TOP OF MY OATMEAL, OR EAT IT ON ITS OWN WITH A SPLASH OF ALMOND MILK OR A FEW SPOONFULS OF *goat's milk yogurt.* IT'S SATISFYING AND VERY *nutritious.* IT'S FREE OF REFINED SUGAR AND OTHER ADDITIVES TOO. NOW THAT'S A *good* BREAKFAST!

PREPARATION
60 MINUTES

INGREDIENTS
- 3 CUPS (250 G) WHOLE OATS
- ⅓ CUP (50 G) WALNUTS
- ⅓ CUP (50 G) HAZELNUTS
- ⅓ CUP (50 G) ALMONDS
- ⅓ CUP (50 G) SUNFLOWER SEEDS
- ⅓ CUP (50 G) SESAME SEEDS
- 2 TABLESPOONS (20 G) OAT BRAN
- 1 TEASPOON SEA SALT
- 1 TABLESPOON (15 ML) HOT WATER
- 1 TEASPOON PURE VANILLA EXTRACT
- ⅝ CUP (200 G) HONEY
- ½ CUP (120 G) COCONUT OIL, MELTED
- ⅓ CUP (50 G) UNSWEETENED DRIED APRICOTS (OPTIONAL)
- ½ CUP (50 G) UNSWEETENED DRIED BANANA SLICES (OPTIONAL)

DIRECTIONS

Preheat the oven to 300°F (160°C). In a large mixing bowl, combine the oats, nuts, seeds, and oat bran. In a small bowl, dissolve the salt in the hot water, then whisk in the vanilla, honey, and melted coconut oil. Add the liquid mixture to the dry ingredients, stirring carefully to coat the dry ingredients evenly.

Transfer the mixture to a parchment-lined baking sheet, spreading it out evenly. Place the baking sheet on the middle rack in the oven and bake for 40 minutes, carefully stirring the mixture every 10 minutes to ensure the entire batch is browned evenly. Turn off the oven, open the oven door about halfway, and allow the granola to cool fully in the oven. Mix in the dried fruit if you're using it. Store the cooled granola in an airtight container.

YIELD: 2¼ POUNDS (1 KG)

Power Food

OATMEAL WITH BANANA AND PLUMS

Oatmeal IS HOT! YOUR BODY DIGESTS IT EASILY, IT KEEPS YOUR *hunger* IN CHECK, AND YOU CAN *combine* IT WITH VIRTUALLY ANY *fruit*, NUT, OR SPICE. THIS RECIPE CALLS FOR BANANA, *coconut*, PLUMS, AND CINNAMON.

PREPARATION
15 MINUTES

INGREDIENTS
- 1½ CUPS (120 G) OATMEAL
- 1 BANANA
- 2½ CUPS (600 ML) ALMOND OR RICE MILK (PAGE 156)
- 2 PINCHES OF GROUND CINNAMON
- 4 PLUMS OR 1 APPLE
- 2 TABLESPOONS (10 G) GRATED COCONUT

DIRECTIONS

Combine the oatmeal, half the banana (mashed) and the almond milk in a saucepan, and bring to a boil. Simmer for 5 minutes. Spice it up by adding the cinnamon. Divide the oatmeal between 2 serving bowls. Slice the plums (or apple) and the remaining banana into bite-size pieces. Top the oatmeal with the fruit and the grated coconut. *Bon appétit!*

YIELD: 2 SERVINGS

"Treat yourself to a good breakfast."

ALMOND-PUMPKIN BREAD

SINCE I DON'T REALLY EAT MUCH BREAD, I LIKE TO USE A *small* LOAF PAN FOR THIS RECIPE (ABOUT 6 INCHES, OR 15 CM). SOMETIMES I'LL MAKE THREE LOAVES AT A TIME, ONE FOR NOW AND TWO TO GO IN THE *freezer*. REALLY HANDY! IF YOU DO REALLY LIKE YOUR *bread,* YOU CAN ALWAYS *double* THE RECIPE AND MAKE ONE LARGER LOAF.

PREPARATION
85 MINUTES

INGREDIENTS
··· 1 SMALL (4-OUNCE, OR 100 G) PUMPKIN
··· 2 TABLESPOONS (40 G) AGAVE SYRUP (OPTIONAL)
··· 1 TEASPOON PURE VANILLA EXTRACT
··· 3 EGGS
··· 1 TABLESPOON (15 G) COCONUT OIL, MELTED, PLUS EXTRA FOR GREASING
··· 1 CUP (120 G) ALMOND FLOUR
··· 1 TEASPOON BAKING POWDER
··· 2 TABLESPOONS (10 G) PUMPKIN SEEDS
··· 1 TABLESPOON (12 G) FLAXSEEDS
··· 1 TEASPOON GROUND CINNAMON
··· ½ TEASPOON SEA SALT

SUPPLIES
BLENDER, 6-INCH (15 CM) CAKE PAN OR LOAF PAN

DIRECTIONS

Preheat the oven to 350°F (180°C). Grease the cake or loaf pan with coconut oil.

Cut the pumpkin in half, remove the seeds, and chop into pieces. Spread the pieces evenly on a baking sheet, toss with a bit of melted coconut oil, and bake for 30 to 40 minutes, until tender. Remove from the oven and let cool.

Once cooled, transfer the pumpkin to the blender and combine with the agave, vanilla, eggs, and coconut oil. Process until smooth. Pour the contents of the blender into a large mixing bowl and stir in the flour, baking powder, pumpkin seeds, flaxseeds, cinnamon, and salt. Spread in the prepared pan. Bake for about 45 minutes, until a toothpick inserted in the center comes out clean.

Serve warm with a bit of nut butter (page 127), or without anything at all—it's moist and delicious all on its own!

YIELD: ONE 6-INCH (15 CM) CAKE OR LOAF

KICK-START

THIS IS PROBABLY THE MOST DELICIOUS AND *healthiest* BREAKFAST EVER! IT'S SO SATISFYING AND IS DELICIOUSLY *creamy*. IT'S THE PERFECT *pre-workout breakfast,* A QUICK SNACK FOR AN ENERGY *boost,* OR THE BEST POSSIBLE "KICK-START" TO A LONG, BUSY DAY.

PREPARATION
AHEAD OF TIME:
OVERNIGHT OR AT LEAST 4 HOURS
ACTIVE PREPARATION:
10 MINUTES

INGREDIENTS
··· 1½ CUPS (130 G) WHOLE OATS
··· ⅔ CUP (100 G) CASHEWS
··· ½ CUP (80 G) DATES
··· 1 TABLESPOON (15 G)
    COCONUT OIL
··· 2 TABLESPOONS (10 G)
    GRATED COCONUT
··· 2 TEASPOONS PURE VANILLA
    EXTRACT

SUPPLIES
BLENDER

DIRECTIONS
Soak the oats and cashews in filtered water overnight or for at least 4 hours (which would require you to get up way too early!). Drain the water and transfer the oats and cashews to the blender. Add the other ingredients and process until creamy. Feel free to garnish your breakfast with a handful of berries.

YIELD: 4 SERVINGS

"*I dance my head empty and my heart full.*"

BREAKFAST QUINOA

A *sweet and sour* BREAKFAST. IT'S *vegan*, BUT BECAUSE OF THE QUINOA, IT'S FULL OF *protein* TO KEEP YOU GOING AND GOING. IT'S A GREAT OPTION WHEN YOU'VE GOT A BUSY DAY AHEAD OF YOU. LAY THE GROUNDWORK FOR A *relaxed* MORNING AND PREPARE THIS ONE THE NIGHT BEFORE AND STORE IT IN THE FRIDGE.

PREPARATION
15 MINUTES

INGREDIENTS
··· ¾ CUP (120 G) QUINOA
··· 1 CUP (240 ML) APPLE JUICE
··· PINCH OF SEA SALT
··· 1 TABLESPOON (15 ML) LEMON JUICE
··· 1 TEASPOON GROUND CINNAMON, PLUS MORE FOR SPRINKLING
··· 2 DROPS STEVIA
··· 1 TABLESPOON (15 G) NUT BUTTER (PAGE 127)
··· CHOPPED WALNUTS AND CHOPPED APPLE OR BLUEBERRIES, FOR SERVING (OPTIONAL)

SUPPLIES
BLENDER OR MIXER

DIRECTIONS

Rinse the quinoa in a sieve and heat the apple juice in a pot over medium-high heat. Add the quinoa and salt, cover, and simmer until the liquid has been absorbed, about 15 minutes. Transfer the quinoa to the blender, add the lemon juice, cinnamon, and stevia, and process until combined. Divide the mixture between 2 bowls and top with a sprinkle of cinnamon, a dollop of nut butter, and some chopped walnuts and apple or blueberries. You can eat it right away or store it in the fridge and eat it cold. Enjoy!

YIELD: 2 SERVINGS

CHIA-BANANA PUDDING

MUCH OF MY *food inspiration* COMES FROM *New York*. WHEN I WAS LIVING IN THE BIG APPLE, I DISCOVERED THIS FANTASTIC BREAKFAST. PUDDING SOUNDS SUGARY AND UNHEALTHY, BUT THIS *version* IS THE OPPOSITE. THIS *nutritious* AND TASTY SWEET DISH IS GOOD FOR YOUR *body* AND IS AN AWESOME WAY TO START THE DAY.

PREPARATION
4 HOURS

INGREDIENTS
··· 1 BANANA
··· 1 CUP (240 ML) ALMOND MILK (PAGE 156)
··· 1 TABLESPOON (20 G) HONEY
··· ½ TEASPOON PURE VANILLA EXTRACT
··· 4 HEAPING TABLESPOONS (50 G) CHIA SEEDS

SUPPLIES
BLENDER

DIRECTIONS

Process the banana, almond milk, honey, and vanilla in the blender until thick and creamy. Transfer the mixture to a cup and add the chia seeds. Stir well so that the seeds are evenly distributed. Cover with plastic wrap, place the cup in the fridge, and cool for at least 4 hours (or overnight). When it's done, I'll often put it in a jar with a layer of jam, nut butter, and goat's milk yogurt. The end result is delicious as a breakfast, but is also great for dessert or a snack.

YIELD: 1 SERVING

NUTS

Nuts are healthy. They are free of gluten and a good source of protein, minerals, and healthy fats. You have more than enough varieties to choose from, including walnuts, almonds, pistachios, hazelnuts, and cashews. Eating a handful of nuts is satisfying, which makes it the perfect snack. I also use them to make piecrusts and cake bottoms. It's always a good plan to stock your pantry with nuts.

SWEET PANCAKES

I *love* SWEETS AND I MAKE SURE TO TREAT MYSELF EVERY SO OFTEN TO A *muffin,* A SLICE OF CAKE, OR PANCAKES FOR BREAKFAST—ESPECIALLY ON *Sunday* MORNINGS. I LOVE TO *spoil* MY SWEETIE (AND MYSELF) WITH AN ELABORATE *brunch.* SO, OF COURSE, I HAD TO THINK UP A *healthy* PANCAKE RECIPE TO RELY ON.

PREPARATION
20 MINUTES

INGREDIENTS
- ⅔ CUP (80 G) QUINOA FLOUR OR BUCKWHEAT FLOUR
- 1½ CUPS (120 G) WHOLE OATS
- 4 EGGS
- 1⅔ CUPS (400 ML) UNSWEETENED RICE MILK
- 2 TABLESPOONS (10 G) GRATED COCONUT
- 1½ TABLESPOONS (20 G) GROUND FLAXSEEDS
- PINCH OF SALT
- COCONUT OIL, FOR COOKING
- TOPPINGS OF CHOICE

SUPPLIES
BLENDER

DIRECTIONS

Add the flour, oats, eggs, rice milk, coconut, flaxseeds, and salt to the blender and process until smooth.

Heat a bit of coconut oil in a frying pan, pour a dollop of batter into the pan, and repeat 5 times. When bubbles appear on the surface, flip and cook on the other side.

I top mine with nut butter, sliced banana, a trickle of maple syrup, a sprinkling of grated coconut, and a small handful of goji berries. Perfect for sharing with your loved one.

YIELD: 6 PANCAKES

Power Food

POPEYE'S BREAKFAST

AT LEAST *once a week,* I START MY DAY WITH THIS GREEN SPINACH SMOOTHIE. IT MIGHT SOUND A BIT CRAZY TO EAT SPINACH FOR BREAKFAST, BUT THESE GREEN LEAVES ARE FULL OF *vitamins* AND MINERALS. THIS BREAKFAST REALLY DOES GIVE YOUR BODY A *shot of health!* SHORT ON TIME IN THE MORNING? MAKE THIS *smoothie* BEFORE YOU GO TO BED AND STORE IT IN A TO-GO CUP IN THE FRIDGE SO YOU CAN GRAB IT AND RUN THE NEXT DAY.

PREPARATION
10 MINUTES

INGREDIENTS
··· ½ BANANA
··· ½ SLICE OF PINEAPPLE
··· ½ APPLE
··· JUICE OF A LIME
··· JUICE OF ½ GRAPEFRUIT
··· JUICE OF 1 ORANGE
··· 1⅓ CUP (40 G) SPINACH
··· 1 TEASPOON CHLORELLA POWDER
··· 1 TABLESPOON PROTEIN POWDER

SUPPLIES
BLENDER

DIRECTIONS

Add the fruit and fruit juices to the blender first, then place the spinach on top and blend until smooth. Add the chlorella and protein powders and process again until fully combined. Looking for more smoothie inspiration? See page 146.

YIELD: 2 CUPS (480 ML)

This cake stays really moist.

BREAKFAST CAKE

IF I KNOW THAT I HAVE A *busy week* AHEAD OF ME, I'LL BAKE THIS CAKE THE *weekend before*. THAT WAY I CAN JUST SLICE OFF A NICE, BIG PIECE EACH MORNING. *Super simple*, SUPER TASTY, AND SUPER NUTRITIOUS. IN SHORT, IT'S THE *perfect* BREAKFAST!

PREPARATION
30 MINUTES

INGREDIENTS
··· 4 EGGS
··· 1 LARGE BANANA
··· 1½ CUPS (120 G) WHOLE OATS
··· 2 TEASPOONS GROUND CINNAMON
··· 1 TEASPOON PURE VANILLA EXTRACT
··· SMALL HANDFUL DRIED MULBERRIES
··· SMALL HANDFUL DRIED GOJI BERRIES

SUPPLIES
BLENDER, 12-INCH (30 CM) CAKE PAN

DIRECTIONS
Preheat the oven to 350°F (180°C) and grease the cake pan with coconut oil. Add all the ingredients, with the exception of the mulberries and goji berries, to the blender and mix until thick and creamy. Transfer the mixture to a large mixing bowl and add the dried fruit. Stir to combine. Pour the batter into the cake pan and place in the oven. Twenty-five minutes later, your cake is done!

YIELD: 4 SERVINGS

Lunch

A lunch break is always a good idea.

A good lunch is very important. If you take the time to eat a nutritious lunch, you can make it through the entire afternoon! You not only supply your body with much-needed energy, but you'll also give yourself a break from your daily activities. Even when I'm busy, I make sure to consciously enjoy my lunch breaks.

QUINOA SUSHI

All you can eat! I'M NOT KIDDING, BECAUSE THIS SUSHI IS INCREDIBLY HEALTHY. TAKE AN *afternoon* TO RELAX AND ROLL SOME SUSHI WITH YOUR LOVER OR YOUR *friends*. THIS SUSHI IS PERFECT WHEN YOU'RE *entertaining,* BUT IT'S ALSO GREAT FOR A *romantic* EVENING MEAL OR AS A POST-WORKOUT SNACK.

PREPARATION
25 MINUTES

INGREDIENTS
- 2 CUPS (200 G) QUINOA
- 1 ORGANIC VEGETABLE
  BOUILLON CUBE
- 6 OUNCES (150 G) ORGANIC TOFU
- 4 OUNCES (100 G) SUSHI-GRADE
  SALMON OR TUNA
- 1 AVOCADO
- ½ CUCUMBER
- 1 LARGE CARROT
- 4 NORI SHEETS
- MAYONNAISE (OPTIONAL, PAGE 132)
- SESAME OIL (OPTIONAL)
- CAYENNE (OPTIONAL)
- 4 TABLESPOONS (60 ML)
  SOY SAUCE
- 4 TEASPOONS WASABI

SUPPLIES
ROLLING MAT, BUT YOU CAN ALSO
MAKE THE SUSHI WITHOUT ONE
(CHALLENGE!)

DIRECTIONS

Rinse the quinoa in a sieve, transfer to a pot, and cook in water with the bouillon cube according to the package instructions. Allow to cool.

In the meantime, give the tofu and fish a rinse and pat dry. Slice the tofu, fish, avocado, cucumber, and carrot into nice, long, thin strips (about the length of the sheets of nori). Place one-fourth of the quinoa on a nori sheet and top with mayonnaise (if using). Lay some strips of tofu, fish, and vegetables close together, lengthwise, on the quinoa-coated nori sheet. Sprinkle with a bit of sesame oil and a bit of cayenne if you like it spicy. Now roll the sushi tightly either by hand or using a rolling mat and wet the edge of the nori at the end to seal the roll. Using a sharp knife, slice the sushi into pieces. Serve the sushi with soy sauce and wasabi.

You can make all sorts of different rolls by using different ingredients. Make it as crazy as you want—it's always fun to experiment!

YIELD: 4 SUSHI ROLLS

CRUNCHY CRACKERS

MAKING YOUR OWN CRACKERS MEANS YOU KNOW EXACTLY WHAT'S IN THEM AND YOU CAN MAKE THEM MORE *nutritious* THAN THE AVERAGE CRACKER OR CRISP BREAD YOU BUY AT THE SUPERMARKET. THEY ALSO JUST TASTE A LOT BETTER! I OFTEN EAT THESE DELICIOUS, CRUNCHY *bread substitutes* FOR LUNCH WITH *hummus* OR HOMEMADE *guacamole*.

PREPARATION
60 MINUTES

INGREDIENTS
- 3 HEAPING TABLESPOONS (15 G) PUMPKIN SEEDS
- 3 HEAPING TABLESPOONS (27 G) SUNFLOWER SEEDS
- 3 HEAPING TABLESPOONS (36 G) FLAXSEEDS
- ½ CUP (72 G) SESAME SEEDS
- 3 HEAPING TABLESPOONS (15 G) PUFFED AMARANTH
- 3 HEAPING TABLESPOONS (15 G) OATMEAL
- ⅔ CUP (80 G) RYE FLOUR
- ¾ CUP (90 G) BUCKWHEAT FLOUR
- 1 TEASPOON BAKING POWDER
- 1½ TEASPOONS SALT
- 2 TABLESPOONS (15 G) COCONUT OIL, MELTED
- ½ CUP (120 ML) WATER

DIRECTIONS
Preheat the oven to 325°F (170°C). Combine all the ingredients, except the water, in a bowl and then slowly add the water, bit by bit, until the dough begins to stick to itself.

Lay a sheet of parchment paper on a baking sheet, place the dough on top, and use a rolling pin to flatten it out. Using a knife, score the dough into small rectangles. Place the baking sheet in the oven and bake for 45 minutes. Serve with homemade hummus (page 128) or another savory spread. Enjoy!

YIELD: 10 CRACKERS

RAINBOW SALAD

KEEPING IN MIND THAT THE MORE *colorful,* UNPROCESSED FOOD WE EAT, THE MORE *nutrients* WE CONSUME, THIS *rainbow* OF A SALAD IS ABOUT AS HEALTHY AS IT GETS. HAVING LOTS OF COLORS ON YOUR PLATE CAN PROMPT YOU TO EAT MORE, BUT THAT'S NOT A PROBLEM WITH THIS SALAD. I'LL OFTEN EAT IT WITH A *cracker* ON THE SIDE.

PREPARATION
40 MINUTES

INGREDIENTS
SALAD
- ¼ CUP (50 G) LENTILS
- 2 CUPS (480 ML) WATER
- SEA SALT, TO TASTE
- 1 LARGE CARROT
- 1 AVOCADO
- 8 CHERRY TOMATOES
- ½ ZUCCHINI
- 2 HEAPING TABLESPOONS (30 G) HOMEMADE HUMMUS (PAGE 128)

SOUR SALAD DRESSING
- 1 TABLESPOON (15 ML) LEMON JUICE
- 1 TEASPOON TAHINI (PAGE 143)
- 1 TEASPOON APPLE CIDER VINEGAR
- 3 TABLESPOONS (45 ML) OLIVE OIL
- 1 TEASPOON HONEY
- SEA SALT AND BLACK PEPPER, TO TASTE

SUPPLIES
SPIRALIZER

DIRECTIONS

To make the salad, place the lentils and the water in a saucepan and bring to a boil over high heat; lower the heat and simmer for 30 to 35 minutes, until tender. Drain the lentils and sprinkle with a pinch of sea salt. Grate the carrot, slice the avocado and tomatoes, and use the spiralizer to slice the zucchini into "noodles." Arrange the vegetables on a large plate or dish as shown in the photo. Spoon the hummus on top, somewhere in the middle.

To make the dressing, combine all the ingredients in a small bowl. Stir well and pour over the tasty, colorful salad. Enjoy your colorful lunch!

YIELD: 1 SERVING

"A healthy, nutritious lunch helps me resist the temptation to eat unhealthy snacks."

BEET SALAD

I CAME UP WITH THIS RECIPE *by accident*. I WAS AT MY PARENTS' HOUSE IN FRIESLAND AND WANTED TO MAKE A *quick salad*. I JUST GRABBED WHATEVER INGREDIENTS I COULD FIND IN THEIR KITCHEN AND CAME UP WITH THIS. IT'S A LOVELY COMBINATION OF *sweet* AND *savory,* AND IT'S QUITE FILLING. NO TIME? BUY *precooked* BEETS AT THE GROCERY STORE, WHICH WILL SAVE YOU A BIT OF PREP.

PREPARATION
60 MINUTES

INGREDIENTS
··· 1 POUND (454 G) SMALL BEETS
··· ²/₃ CUP (100 G) RED QUINOA
··· 1 ORGANIC BOUILLON CUBE
··· 1 SHALLOT
··· 2 TEASPOONS CHOPPED ROSEMARY
··· 2 TEASPOONS TURMERIC
··· SEA SALT AND BLACK PEPPER, TO TASTE
··· 3 CLOVES GARLIC
··· ½ INCH (1 CM) GINGER
··· 1 CUP (150 G) CUBED FETA
··· 3 SPRIGS FRESH THYME
··· SMALL HANDFUL WALNUTS, CHOPPED
··· 1 SCANT TABLESPOON (20 G) HONEY

SUPPLIES
MORTAR AND PESTLE

DIRECTIONS

Scrub the beets, place in a saucepan, and cover with water. Bring to a boil over high heat, lower the heat, and cook for about 40 minutes, until tender when pierced with a knife. Drain and allow to cool. Meanwhile, rinse the quinoa in a sieve, transfer to a pot, and cook in water with the bouillon cube according to the package instructions. Set aside and allow to cool. Next, chop the beets and the shallot and combine with the rosemary, turmeric, salt, and pepper in a bowl. Press the garlic and ginger into the bowl using a garlic press. Crumble the feta into the bowl. Mix together using a large spoon. Use the mortar and pestle to smash the thyme sprigs and, along with the walnuts, sprinkle on top of the salad. Add a little sweetness to the salad by drizzling it with a bit of honey.

YIELD: 4 SERVINGS

BEETS

I eat beets quite often and always have them on hand. Raw, cooked, warm, or cold, they are a versatile and healthy vegetable. I make beet juice with them. They add sweetness and a fantastic color to my juices. You can also make them into soup or add them to a salad.

WRAPS WITH CURRIED CHICKEN SALAD

CURRIED CHICKEN SALAD ISN'T THE HEALTHIEST *spread* IN THE WORLD . . . UNLESS YOU MAKE IT YOURSELF WITH HEALTHY INGREDIENTS. FATTY MAYONNAISE IS NOT REQUIRED. THIS SPREAD IS *super tasty* ON A RICE CAKE, AS WELL AS IN THESE *wraps*. MAKE THESE AS A *lovely lunch* FOR YOURSELF OR AS A FUN SNACK TO SHARE.

PREPARATION
30 MINUTES

INGREDIENTS
··· 12 OUNCES (300 G) ORGANIC
    CHICKEN BREAST
··· 1 TEASPOON CURRY POWDER
··· 1 TEASPOON TURMERIC
··· 1 TEASPOON GARLIC POWDER
··· 1 TEASPOON LAOS POWDER
··· 1 TABLESPOON (15 ML)
    COLD-PRESSED OLIVE OIL
··· ½ ONION
··· 6 OUNCES (150 G) MUSHROOMS
··· 6 OUNCES (150 G) CHERRY
    TOMATOES
··· ½ CUP (7 G) FRESH CILANTRO
··· COCONUT OIL, FOR COOKING
··· 2 AVOCADOS
··· 1 TABLESPOON (15 G) ORGANIC
    GOAT'S MILK YOGURT
··· 2 CLOVES GARLIC
··· HIMALAYAN SALT AND BLACK
    PEPPER, TO TASTE
··· 8 STURDY LETTUCE LEAVES
··· 8 SMALL PICKLES, FOR GARNISH

DIRECTIONS

Rinse the chicken breast with water and pat dry. Combine the spices and olive oil in a bowl, add the chicken, and marinate the chicken while you prepare the rest of the ingredients. Chop the onion and mushrooms into small pieces, halve the cherry tomatoes, and finely chop the cilantro.

Coat a skillet with coconut oil, add the chicken and the mushrooms, and panfry until the chicken is cooked through and no longer pink. Once cooked, finely chop the chicken.

Peel and pit the avocados, scoop out the flesh into a large bowl, and add the yogurt, onion, and chicken. Press the garlic into the bowl using a garlic press and mix well. Add the mushrooms, tomatoes, and cilantro, and combine thoroughly. Season to taste with Himalayan salt and black pepper. Spoon the chicken salad onto the lettuce leaves and top each with a pickle.

YIELD: 8 WRAPS

Serve with an extra dish of soy sauce so that you can dip your sushi in it.

SUSHI HAND ROLLS WITH HOMEMADE HUMMUS

Traditional SUSHI HAND ROLLS FOR LUNCH ARE A HEALTHY ALTERNATIVE TO YOUR USUAL CHEESE SANDWICH. YOU CAN EASILY MAKE THIS JAPANESE DISH YOURSELF AND IT'S EVEN *tastier* WITH THE ADDITION OF *homemade hummus.* I'LL OFTEN BRING THESE ROLLS WITH ME FOR LUNCH, BUT YOU CAN ALSO *keep* THEM IN THE FRIDGE AS A *go-to snack.*

PREPARATION
30 MINUTES

INGREDIENTS
··· 1 CUP (200 G) BROWN RICE
··· 1 VEGETABLE BOUILLON CUBE
··· ½ CARROT
··· ½ AVOCADO
··· ¼ CUCUMBER
··· 4 NORI SHEETS
··· 4 TABLESPOONS (60 G) HOMEMADE HUMMUS (PAGE 128)
··· 4 TEASPOONS (20 ML) SOY SAUCE, PLUS EXTRA FOR DIPPING
··· SEA SALT AND BLACK PEPPER, TO TASTE
··· 1 TABLESPOON (8 G) SESAME SEEDS

DIRECTIONS
Cook the rice in water with the bouillon cube according to package directions until the rice is sticky. Meanwhile, julienne the carrot, avocado, and cucumber into long, thin strips. Lay a nori sheet diagonally on a plate, with the shiny side facing down. Spoon 2 tablespoons (30 g) of cooked rice diagonally in the middle of the nori sheet, followed by equal amounts of each vegetable, a tablespoon (15 g) of hummus, and a teaspoon (5 ml) of soy sauce. Season to taste with salt and pepper, and roll the nori sheet up in the form of an ice cream cone, starting on the left side. Repeat this process until you've used up all the ingredients. Sprinkle with sesame seeds, wrap the sushi in plastic wrap, and you're done!

YIELD: 4 SUSHI HAND ROLLS

SAVORY PANCAKE

I *love* PANCAKES, AND NOT JUST THE SWEET ONES WITH *fruit* AND SYRUP, BUT SAVORY ONES TOO! I'LL USE THEM WARM OR *cold* TO MAKE A WRAP. THERE ARE *endless* VARIATIONS, BUT THIS VERSION WITH *goat's milk cheese,* PESTO, AND SAMBAL (CHILI PEPPER SAUCE) IS MY *favorite.*

PREPARATION
45 MINUTES

INGREDIENTS
PANCAKE
- 5 TABLESPOONS (40 G) BUCKWHEAT FLOUR, QUINOA FLOUR, OR SPELT FLOUR
- PINCH OF HIMALAYAN SALT OR SEA SALT
- 1 EGG
- 4 TABLESPOONS (60 ML) ALMOND MILK (PAGE 156)
- 1 TABLESPOON (15 G) COCONUT OIL

FILLING
- 1 LARGE SLICE HARD GOAT'S MILK CHEESE
- 2 TEASPOONS PESTO (PAGE 131)
- 2 LARGE LEAVES ICEBERG LETTUCE
- 6 CHERRY TOMATOES, SLICED
- 2 TEASPOONS YELLOW SAMBAL (PAGE 142)
- SALT AND BLACK PEPPER, TO TASTE

SUPPLIES
WHISK OR MIXER

DIRECTIONS

To make the pancake, whisk the flour and a pinch of salt together in a bowl. Make a well in the middle of the flour and crack the egg into it. Add the almond milk and combine with a whisk or a hand mixer until the batter is smooth. Let the batter rest for 30 minutes. Warm the coconut oil in a frying pan and pour the batter in. Cook the pancake for about 3 minutes over medium-high heat until the underside is lightly browned and the top is dry. Flip the pancake using a spatula and cook the other side for about 1 minute, until golden brown. Transfer the pancake to a plate and allow it to cool for 5 to 10 minutes.

For the filling, top the cool pancake with the goat's milk cheese, pesto, lettuce, and tomatoes, and season with the sambal, salt, and black pepper to taste. Roll up the pancake and enjoy!

YIELD: 1 SERVING

"Food lovers are life lovers."

QUINOA SALAD

WHEN I MAKE A SALAD, I TEND TO LET MY *imagination* RUN WILD. QUINOA, IN PARTICULAR, CAN BE COMBINED WITH JUST ABOUT ANYTHING, BUT THIS *combo* IS MY FAVORITE. IT'S *super quick* TO MAKE AND, IN THE *summer*, IT'S A GREAT CHOICE TO BRING WITH YOU TO A PICNIC IN THE *park*.

PREPARATION
35 MINUTES

INGREDIENTS
··· 1 CUP (180 G) QUINOA
··· 1¼ CUPS (300 ML) WATER
··· 1 VEGETABLE BOUILLON CUBE
··· ¾ CUCUMBER
··· 8 OUNCES (200 G) CHERRY
    TOMATOES
··· 1 AVOCADO
··· 1 SPRING ONION
··· 1 SMALL RED ONION
··· 2 CLOVES GARLIC
··· 4 TABLESPOONS (32 G)
    CHOPPED OLIVES
··· 1 CUP (150 G) CRUMBLED FETA
··· 3 TABLESPOONS (3 G) FINELY
    CHOPPED CILANTRO
··· SALT AND BLACK PEPPER,
    TO TASTE
··· 1 TEASPOON LEMON JUICE
··· 1 TABLESPOON (15 ML) OLIVE OIL
··· SMALL HANDFUL ARUGULA

DIRECTIONS
Rinse the quinoa in a sieve, add to a saucepan along with the water and bouillon, cover, and cook according to package directions until tender, about 15 minutes. Allow to cool. Chop the cucumber, tomatoes, avocado, and onions into small pieces and press the garlic using a garlic press. In a large bowl, combine the quinoa with the vegetables, garlic, olives, feta, and cilantro. Season to taste with salt and pepper, and sprinkle with the lemon juice and olive oil. Mix well using a spoon. Finally, add the arugula. The salad can be served immediately or stored in the fridge for later.

YIELD: 4 SERVINGS

Dinner

Good things take time.

I like to eat light at dinner, as your metabolism runs a bit more slowly in the evening. In any case, it's a good idea to eat a nutritious meal, especially when you've had a busy day. I don't just curl up on the couch after a long day; I get in the kitchen and focus on making a tasty dinner.

SAOTO SOUP

DESPITE THE FACT THAT I'M *Frisian*, BORN AND BRED, I ADORE *exotic* DISHES. THIS SOUP HAS ITS ORIGINS IN *Java* AND IS MADE OFTEN IN SURINAMESE CUISINE. WHEN I WAS YOUNG, I USED TO HAVE DINNER WITH A SURINAMESE FAMILY EVERY NOW AND THEN, AND THAT'S WHERE I DISCOVERED SAOTO SOUP. YOU CAN MAKE THIS SOUP AS *filling* AND AS *spicy* AS YOU'D LIKE.

PREPARATION
60 MINUTES

INGREDIENTS
- 3 ORGANIC CHICKEN BREASTS
- 2 QUARTS (2 L) WATER
- 1 ONION
- 4 CLOVES GARLIC
- 1 ORGANIC VEGETABLE BOUILLON CUBE
- 2 ORGANIC CHICKEN BOUILLON CUBES
- 2 BAY LEAVES
- 1 TABLESPOON (15 ML) KETJAP MANIS (SWEET SOY SAUCE)
- 1 TEASPOON LAOS POWDER
- ½ TEASPOON GROUND GINGER
- SEA SALT AND BLACK PEPPER, TO TASTE
- ½ CUP (80 G) BASMATI RICE
- 4 HARD-BOILED EGGS
- 6 OUNCES (150 G) BEAN SPROUTS
- 1 TEASPOON DRIED PARSLEY
- 1 TEASPOON YELLOW SAMBAL (OPTIONAL, PAGE 142)

DIRECTIONS

Put the chicken breasts in a pot and add the water. Coarsely chop the onion and mince the garlic, and add both to the pot. Add the bouillon cubes, bay leaves, ketjap, Laos powder, and ground ginger. Season with salt and pepper. Bring the mixture to a boil, then lower the heat, cover, and simmer for at least an hour, until a flavorful broth has formed. After about an hour, remove the chicken breasts and pull the meat into pieces using two forks. In the meantime, cook the rice according to the package instructions and cut the eggs into quarters. Put a bit of rice, topped with bean sprouts and chicken, in the middle of each soup bowl. Pour the soup on top and position the egg quarters around the edges of the bowl. Sprinkle with the dried parsley and pepper. You can always add a bit of yellow sambal (page 142) for some heat. You can also serve with delicious, thin sweet potato fries (page 95). Always good!

YIELD: 4 SERVINGS

STUFFED PORTOBELLO MUSHROOMS

THIS IS THE *perfect* DINNER PARTY APPETIZER THAT IS GUARANTEED TO *impress*. AND DON'T TELL ANYONE, BUT I'VE ALSO BEEN KNOWN TO MAKE THESE STUFFED PORTOBELLO MUSHROOMS ON A *weekday evening,* JUST BECAUSE. MY BOYFRIEND AND I SHARE THEM FOR DINNER AND I REHEAT THE LEFTOVERS FOR *lunch* THE NEXT DAY.

PREPARATION
30 MINUTES

INGREDIENTS
- 1 CUP (150 G) BUCKWHEAT GROATS
- 2 CUPS (480 ML) WATER
- 1 ORGANIC CHICKEN BOUILLON CUBE
- 6 PORTOBELLO MUSHROOMS
- OLIVE OIL, FOR DRIZZLING
- 1 RED ONION
- 3 CLOVES GARLIC
- 1 TEASPOON COCONUT OIL
- 1 TABLESPOON (15 ML) ORGANIC WHITE WINE
- 3/4 CUP (100 G) PEAS
- 1 HEAPING TEASPOON OREGANO
- 2 TABLESPOONS (30 G) PESTO (PAGE 131)
- SEA SALT AND BLACK PEPPER, TO TASTE
- HARD GOAT'S MILK CHEESE
- 6 BASIL LEAVES

SUPPLIES
OVENPROOF DISH

DIRECTIONS

Rinse the buckwheat groats in a sieve and transfer to a small pot. Add the water and the bouillon cube. Bring to a boil, cover, lower the heat, and simmer until the water has been absorbed, about 30 minutes. In the meantime, preheat the oven by turning on the highest broiler setting. Clean the mushrooms and remove the hard stems. Lay them in the ovenproof dish, rounded side down, and drizzle with olive oil. Broil for 8 minutes, turning the mushrooms over after 4 minutes. Chop the onion and garlic, and sauté in coconut oil in a skillet over low heat for about 2 minutes. Add the wine, cooked buckwheat groats, peas, oregano, pesto, and salt and pepper to taste. Stir to combine and continue cooking for another couple of minutes. Taste and adjust the seasoning if desired. Position the mushrooms on a serving dish, top each with 2 tablespoons (30 g) of the buckwheat mixture, some grated goat's milk cheese, a drizzle of olive oil, and a basil leaf. Ready to serve!

YIELD: 6 STUFFED MUSHROOMS

MUSHROOMS

Mushrooms are a flavorful addition to meals and contain important nutrients like iron and calcium. You can grill them, sauté them, and stew them. Mushrooms are also a source of protein, which is why they are a great substitute for meat. Good to know: mushrooms aren't vegetables, they're a fungus— a healthy fungus, though!

PUMPKIN SOUP

PUMPKIN IS A QUINTESSENTIAL *autumn vegetable*. WHEN IT'S IN SEASON, IT'S EVERYWHERE. THE VEGETABLE IS *sweet* AND SOFT, COOKS QUICKLY, AND IS EXTREMELY *versatile*. I'LL OFTEN ADD IT TO *risotto*, MAKE IT INTO A PUREE, OR ADD IT TO A CASSEROLE. BUT ON A *rainy*, FALL DAY, THERE'S NOTHING I LIKE MORE THAN GETTING IN THE KITCHEN AND MAKING A BIG POT OF PUMPKIN SOUP.

PREPARATION
40 MINUTES

INGREDIENTS
- 1 RED ONION
- 3 CLOVES GARLIC
- 1 TABLESPOON (15 G) COCONUT OIL
- 1½ QUARTS (1½ L) WATER
- 2 VEGETABLE BOUILLON CUBES
- ONE 3⅓-POUND (1½ KG) PUMPKIN
- 1 ZUCCHINI
- 2 TEASPOONS CURRY POWDER
- PINCH OF POWDERED GINGER
- PINCH OF CAYENNE
- PINCH OF LAOS POWDER
- 1 TEASPOON OREGANO
- SPLASH OF ORGANIC SPELT MILK PER BOWL
- 4 TABLESPOONS (4 G) FINELY CHOPPED CILANTRO
- YELLOW SAMBAL (OPTIONAL, PAGE 142)

SUPPLIES
IMMERSION BLENDER

DIRECTIONS

Chop the red onion and garlic. Sauté the onion in a bit of coconut oil in a skillet over low heat. After a minute, add the garlic and continue to cook. Meanwhile, put a pot on the stove and add the water and bouillon cubes. Peel, seed, and chop the pumpkin into small pieces, chop the zucchini into small pieces, and add both to the pot of bouillon. Add the curry powder, ginger, cayenne, Laos powder, and oregano to the onions and garlic, and sauté for another 30 seconds, stirring well. Add this mixture to the now simmering bouillon and continue to cook the vegetables for about 30 minutes. Once the vegetables are cooked, use the immersion blender to puree the soup. Ladle the soup into bowls. Add a splash of spelt milk to each bowl and top with the chopped cilantro. I always add a tiny bit of yellow sambal to my bowl, but that's only for the die-hard spicy fans!

YIELD: 4 SERVINGS

MISO SOUP

THIS IS A VERY *healthy*, TASTY, *Japanese* RECIPE. MISO PASTE ADDS ITS OWN PARTICULAR FLAVOR AND *kelp* IS ANOTHER IMPORTANT INGREDIENT. SEAWEED IS ABOUT THE HEALTHIEST THING OUT THERE, BUT NOT EVERYONE LIKES ITS TASTE. I THOUGHT UP THIS *veggie-packed* VERSION MYSELF AND WILL HAPPILY *slurp* AWAY A BIG BOWL OF IT IN ONE SITTING.

PREPARATION
40 MINUTES

INGREDIENTS
- 5 PIECES DRIED KOMBU (KELP)
- 2 QUARTS (2 L) WATER
- 6 TABLESPOONS (90 G) SHIRO MISO PASTE
- ½ SWEET POTATO
- 1½ CARROTS
- ½ ZUCCHINI
- 2 CUPS (175 G) MUSHROOMS
- 3 SPRING ONIONS, FINELY SLICED
- 4 CLOVES GARLIC
- 4 TEASPOONS (20 ML) SOY SAUCE (OPTIONAL)

DIRECTIONS

Soak the pieces of kombu in water to cover for 10 minutes. Fill a pot with the 2 quarts (2 L) water, add the shiro miso paste, and bring to a boil. Meanwhile, chop the sweet potato, carrots, zucchini, and mushrooms into small pieces and add them to the pot along with the spring onions. Using a garlic press, press the garlic into the pot. Remove the kombu from the water and chop it into small pieces. Add the kombu to the pot as well. Simmer the soup for about 30 minutes over low heat. Serve in nice bowls with a teaspoon of soy sauce, if you'd like. Ready to eat!

YIELD: 4 SERVINGS

ZUCCHINI BOATS

THIS *creative* ZUCCHINI DISH LOOKS SO *fantastic!* I OFTEN MAKE IT WHEN MY NEPHEW COMES FOR DINNER. IF THE FOOD ON YOUR PLATE LOOKS GOOD AND IS *colorful,* YOU'LL AUTOMATICALLY EAT MORE OF IT. AND IN THIS CASE, YOU DON'T HAVE TO FEEL GUILTY ABOUT EATING *lots,* AS THESE ZUCCHINI BOATS ARE *super* HEALTHY!

PREPARATION
30 MINUTES

INGREDIENTS
- 1 POUND (450 G) ORGANIC CHICKEN BREAST
- 1 TABLESPOON (15 G) COCONUT OIL
- ¾ CUP (120 G) BROWN RICE
- 1 ORGANIC BOUILLON CUBE
- 2 ZUCCHINI
- 1 TABLESPOON (15 ML) OLIVE OIL
- 2 SMALL RED ONIONS
- 8 LARGE MUSHROOMS
- ½ BUNCH PARSLEY
- 12 BASIL LEAVES
- LEAVES OF 4 SPRIGS THYME
- 2 TEASPOONS CURRY POWDER
- 1 TEASPOON TURMERIC
- 1 TEASPOON LAOS POWDER
- 2 PINCHES OF CAYENNE PEPPER
- 3 TABLESPOONS (45 ML) TOMATO SAUCE (PAGE 134)
- SEA SALT AND BLACK PEPPER, TO TASTE
- 3 CLOVES GARLIC

SUPPLIES
OVENPROOF DISH

DIRECTIONS

Preheat the oven to 350°F (180°C). Rinse the chicken breast and cut it into small pieces. Heat the coconut oil in a frying pan and cook the chicken fully over low heat. Stir well from time to time. Rinse the rice and cook it in a pot with water and the bouillon cube following package directions. In the meantime, cut the zucchini in half lengthwise. Scoop out the flesh (reserve in a bowl) and brush the 4 hollow zucchini halves with the olive oil. Place them in an ovenproof dish and bake for about 10 minutes. Next, chop the onions, mushrooms, parsley, and basil and add to the zucchini flesh in the bowl. Then add the cooked chicken, thyme, spices, tomato sauce, and salt and pepper to taste. Press the garlic over the bowl using a garlic press. Stir to combine well. Remove the hollow zucchini halves from the oven and spoon the filling into the "boats." Put the filled boats back in the oven for another 10 minutes. Remove from the oven and sprinkle 2 tablespoons (20 g) of cooked rice over each zucchini half.

YIELD: 4 SERVINGS

GOOD NOODLES

Soba noodles ARE MADE WITH BUCKWHEAT FLOUR, SO THEY'RE EXTRA RICH IN MINERALS AND *protein*. ADD SOME ORGANIC *shrimp,* SEA BEANS (SAMPHIRE), AND LOTS OF SPICE, AND YOU'VE GOT YOURSELF A VERY *tasty* ASIAN DISH.

PREPARATION
30 MINUTES

INGREDIENTS
- 2 CUPS (200 G) SNOW PEAS
- 1½ QUARTS (1½ L) WATER
- 1 ORGANIC BOUILLON CUBE
- 8 OUNCES (200 G) SOBA NOODLES
- 1 TABLESPOON (15 ML) SESAME OIL
- 1 TABLESPOON (8 G) MINCED GINGER
- 1 SPRING ONION, CHOPPED
- 1 RED ONION, CHOPPED
- 4 CLOVES GARLIC, MINCED
- 12 OUNCES (300 G) ORGANIC PEELED SHRIMP
- 7 TABLESPOONS (7 G) CHOPPED FRESH CILANTRO
- 2 OUNCES (50 G) SEA BEANS (SAMPHIRE)
- 1 TEASPOON TURMERIC
- SEA SALT AND BLACK PEPPER, TO TASTE
- ½ TABLESPOON AGAVE SYRUP
- 1 TABLESPOON (15 ML) TAMARI
- 1 TABLESPOON (8 G) SESAME SEEDS
- ½ LIME

DIRECTIONS

Cook the snow peas in a pot of boiling water for about 10 minutes. In the meantime, boil the 1½ quarts (1½ L) water for the soba noodles, add the bouillon cube, and cook the noodles for about 10 minutes over low heat. Remove the peas from the heat and drain. When the noodles are cooked, drain them using a sieve and rinse with warm water. Heat the sesame oil in a frying pan, add the ginger, onions, and garlic, and sauté for a few minutes. Heat the shrimp in a separate pan with a little sesame oil for a minute or so, and then add them to the onion mixture along with the snow peas, cilantro, sea beans, cooked noodles, turmeric, and a bit of salt and pepper. Add the agave syrup, tamari, and sesame seeds, and stir well. If you'd like, press another clove of garlic into the mixture and sprinkle with the juice of ½ lime. And there you have it! A healthy Asian recipe! *Màn màn chi!*

YIELD: 4 SERVINGS

"Healthy eating starts with the right ingredients."

ZUCCHETTI "PASTA"

THIS IS A *creamy,* FRESH, AND SATISFYING *pasta salad* . . . BUT THE "PASTA" I USE IS MADE OF *zucchini.* IT'S A LOT LIGHTER THAN THE *doughy* ORIGINAL AND IT GIVES YOU MORE *energy.* YOU CAN MAKE ZUCCHINI PASTA SUPER EASILY USING A SPIRALIZER.

PREPARATION
30 MINUTES

INGREDIENTS
SALAD
··· 14 OUNCES (360 G) ORGANIC
   CHICKEN BREAST
··· 1 RED ONION
··· 3 CUPS (200 G) MUSHROOMS
··· 1 TABLESPOON (15 G) COCONUT OIL
··· 2 CLOVES GARLIC
··· ½ CUP (20 G) BASIL LEAVES
··· 15 CHERRY TOMATOES
··· SEA SALT AND BLACK PEPPER,
   TO TASTE
··· 1 CUP (20 G) ARUGULA
··· 1 CUP (150 G) CORN
··· 2 ZUCCHINI

SAUCE
··· ¼ CUP (60 ML) GOAT'S CREAM
··· 1 AVOCADO, PEELED, PITTED, AND
   FLESH SCOOPED OUT
··· 1 TABLESPOON (15 ML) TAMARI

SUPPLIES
SPIRALIZER, IMMERSION BLENDER

DIRECTIONS

To make the salad, rinse and pat the chicken breast dry. Chop the red onion and mushrooms into small pieces. Cook the chicken in a frying pan in the coconut oil over low heat, adding the onion and mushrooms during the last 10 minutes. Using a garlic press, press the garlic into the pan. Be sure to turn the chicken every now and then. Using a spiralizer, slice the zucchini into long, thin, spaghetti-like strips and transfer the "noodles" to a bowl. Finely chop the basil and halve the cherry tomatoes. Add both to the noodles. Add the chicken with the onion, garlic, mushrooms, arugula, and corn to the zucchini salad, and season with sea salt and black pepper.

YIELD: 4 SERVINGS

STUFFED EGGPLANT

THIS *vegetarian* RECIPE IS EASY TO MAKE AND IT LOOKS *delicious*. YOU'LL IMPRESS YOUR FRIENDS, FAMILY, OR *guests* WITH THIS DISH. BUT SOMETIMES, I JUST MAKE THIS DISH ALL FOR MYSELF FOR *dinner*.

PREPARATION
65 MINUTES

INGREDIENTS
- 2 EGGPLANTS
- COCONUT OIL, FOR COOKING
- 2 SMALL RED ONIONS
- ½ ZUCCHINI
- 6 SMALL VINE-RIPENED TOMATOES
- 6 MUSHROOMS
- 1 TEASPOON LAOS POWDER
- 1 TEASPOON TURMERIC
- 4 CLOVES GARLIC, PRESSED
- ¾ CUP (120 G) CRUMBLED FETA
- 2 TABLESPOONS (30 G) PESTO (PAGE 131)
- 2 TABLESPOONS (30 ML) EXTRA VIRGIN OLIVE OIL

DIRECTIONS

Preheat the oven to 350°F (180°C). Remove the stems and slice the eggplants in half lengthwise. Cook the eggplants on both sides in a frying pan in coconut oil until softened. Remove from the heat and scoop the flesh out of the eggplant halves into a large bowl to make room for the filling. Finely chop the onions, zucchini, tomatoes, and mushrooms, add the vegetables to the bowl, and combine with the spices, garlic, feta, and pesto. Stir the filling to combine and spoon into the hollowed-out eggplant halves. Drizzle the halves with the olive oil, place them on a baking sheet, and bake for 45 minutes, until cooked through.

YIELD: 4 SERVINGS

PASTA WITH SALMON

PASTA CAN BE *nutritious* AND GIVE YOU *energy,* ESPECIALLY WHEN IT'S *spelt pasta,* MADE FROM A *grain* THAT'S A BIT FRIENDLIER TO YOUR BODY. AFTER AN INTENSE DAY, I LIKE TO MAKE THIS *tasty* PASTA JUST FOR MYSELF OR FOR *friends* THAT COME OVER FOR DINNER.

PREPARATION
30 MINUTES

INGREDIENTS
- ··· 4 SALMON FILLETS (ABOUT 6 OUNCES, OR 150 G, EACH)
- ··· 3 CLOVES GARLIC, PRESSED, DIVIDED
- ··· SEA SALT AND BLACK PEPPER, TO TASTE
- ··· 2 TEASPOONS THYME
- ··· 4 TABLESPOONS (60 ML) OLIVE OIL, DIVIDED
- ··· 1 POUND (450 G) SPELT PASTA
- ··· 1 ZUCCHINI
- ··· 8 CHERRY TOMATOES
- ··· 2 SMALL RED ONIONS
- ··· 3 TABLESPOONS (45 G) GOAT'S MILK CREAM CHEESE

DIRECTIONS

Rinse the salmon and pat dry. Combine 2 cloves of the pressed garlic, sea salt and pepper, thyme, and 1 tablespoon (15 ml) of the olive oil in a baking dish. Add the salmon and turn to coat in the marinade. Cook the spelt pasta according to the package instructions, and chop all the vegetables in the meantime. Add the remaining 3 tablespoons (45 ml) olive oil to a pan and sauté the vegetables for 5 minutes over high heat. Drain the pasta and return it to the same pot, adding the goat cream cheese and the remaining 1 pressed clove of garlic. Stir well and add the sautéed vegetables.

Fry the salmon in the vegetable pan over low heat until pink, about 3 minutes each side. Slice the cooked salmon into large pieces and add to the pasta and vegetables. Serve in nice bowls. Enjoy!

YIELD: 4 SERVINGS

LASAGNETTE

EVEN IF YOU SWEAR BY THE *traditional* VERSION, YOU'LL LOVE THIS ONE. MY BOYFRIEND LOVES LASAGNA WITH MEAT, BUT WHEN I SERVED HIM THIS VEGETARIAN *variation*, HE WAS *positively* SURPRISED. WHAT'S MORE, THIS LASAGNETTE IS MUCH *lighter* THAN TRADITIONAL LASAGNA, SO YOU DON'T HAVE TO FEEL GUILTY ABOUT EATING A *second helping*.

PREPARATION
25 MINUTES

INGREDIENTS
··· ¾ ZUCCHINI
··· 1 SMALL RED ONION
··· 7 MUSHROOMS
··· 2 CLOVES GARLIC
··· 1 TABLESPOON (15 G) COCONUT OIL
··· 1½ CUPS (350 G) TOMATO SAUCE (PAGE 134)
··· 1 EGG
··· 1 TEASPOON SEA SALT
··· 1 TEASPOON BLACK PEPPER
··· 1 TEASPOON LAOS POWDER
··· 1 TEASPOON CURRY POWDER
··· 1 TEASPOON TURMERIC
··· PINCH OF CAYENNE
··· ½ CUP (65 G) SOFT GOAT CHEESE, DIVIDED
··· OLIVE OIL, FOR GREASING
··· 1 TOMATO
··· SMALL HANDFUL OF FRESH PARSLEY, FOR GARNISH

SUPPLIES
OVENPROOF DISH (ABOUT 12" X 12", OR 30 X 30 CM)

DIRECTIONS

Preheat the oven to 350°F (180°C). Thinly slice the zucchini lengthwise into "sheets" and chop the onion, mushrooms, and garlic. Warm the coconut oil in a frying pan and sauté the onion, mushrooms, and garlic for about 3 minutes. Add the tomato sauce, egg, spices, and a scant tablespoon (8 g) of the goat cheese. Stir and simmer for about 5 minutes. Grease an ovenproof dish with olive oil, chop the tomato, and lay the first layer of zucchini "sheets" in the dish. Make layers, alternating between zucchini, chopped tomato, sauce, and a sprinkling of goat cheese, in that order. Bake the lasagnette for about 15 minutes, until tender. Sprinkle with the chopped parsley before serving.

YIELD: 2 SERVINGS

Tip! This soup is also great with a splash of soy cream and vegetarian sausage!

"SNERT" À LA RENS (SPLIT PEA SOUP)

Split peas, THE MAIN INGREDIENT IN THIS SOUP, ARE FULL OF *protein,* WHICH MEANS THIS TRADITIONAL DUTCH RECIPE IS SUPER HEALTHY—IF YOU MAKE IT *fresh,* THAT IS. AFTER SPENDING AN ENTIRE DAY TRYING TO ACHIEVE THE *perfect* "SNERT" À LA RENS, I FINALLY CAME UP WITH THIS SWEET, SAVORY, AND A TINY BIT *spicy* SOUP. MAKING THIS SOUP IS A GREAT WAY TO SPEND A *wintry* SUNDAY AFTERNOON, AND EATING IT IS THE PERFECT WAY TO SPEND A WINTRY SUNDAY EVENING.

PREPARATION
80 MINUTES

INGREDIENTS
- 3 QUARTS (3 L) WATER
- 2 ORGANIC BOUILLON CUBES
- 1 POUND (450 G) SPLIT PEAS
- 2 BAY LEAVES
- 1 LARGE CARROT
- 1 SWEET POTATO, PEELED
- 1 LARGE ONION
- 3 GREEN ONIONS
- 12-OUNCE (300 G) CELERIAC
- SMALL HANDFUL OF PARSLEY
- 3 CLOVES GARLIC
- ½ CUP (120 G) CANNED CANNELLINI BEANS, RINSED AND DRAINED
- 1 TEASPOON TURMERIC
- 1 TEASPOON CAYENNE
- 1 TEASPOON CURRY POWDER
- 2 SPRIGS THYME
- 6 SPRIGS CHIVE, FINELY CHOPPED

SUPPLIES
BLENDER OR IMMERSION BLENDER
(OPTIONAL)

DIRECTIONS
Add the water, bouillon cubes, split peas, and bay leaves to a large pot, bring to a boil, and simmer for 30 minutes, until the split peas are cooked. Meanwhile, chop the carrot, sweet potato, onion, green onions, celeriac, and parsley. Press the garlic using a garlic press. Add the vegetables and spices (with the exception of the chives) to the pot after the split peas and cook for an additional 45 minutes over low heat. Remove the bay leaves and thyme sprigs, and puree the soup in a blender, if desired. Serve the wintry soup in bowls, topped with the finely chopped chives.

YIELD: 6 TO 8 SERVINGS

CASSEROLE

WHEN IT'S COLD OUTSIDE, THERE'S NOTHING I LIKE MORE THAN *experimenting* WITH STEWS AND CASSEROLES. THIS ONE IS MY *favorite!* IT'S FILLING BUT NOT TOO HEAVY. I USUALLY MAKE IT *during the day* WHEN I HAVE SOME TIME ON MY HANDS SO THAT IT'S READY TO PUT IN THE *oven* IN THE EVENING.

PREPARATION
20 MINUTES

INGREDIENTS
- 1 TABLESPOON (15 G) COCONUT OIL, PLUS MORE FOR GREASING
- 3 LARGE SWEET POTATOES, PEELED
- ½ LARGE RED ONION
- 1 HEAD CAULIFLOWER
- 1 POUND (450 G) COD
- 2 TEASPOONS CURRY POWDER
- SEA SALT AND BLACK PEPPER, TO TASTE
- 3 CLOVES GARLIC
- ⅞ CUP (200 ML) SPELT CREAM
- 2 ORGANIC VEGETABLE BOUILLON CUBES

SUPPLIES
OVENPROOF DISH (8" X 10", OR 20 X 25 CM)

DIRECTIONS

Preheat the oven to 350°F (180°C) and grease the ovenproof dish with a bit of coconut oil. Thinly slice the sweet potatoes lengthwise. Chop the onion and cauliflower into small pieces. Clean the fish and place in a bowl. Sprinkle the fish with the curry powder, a pinch of salt, and some black pepper. Using a garlic press, press the garlic over the top. Place half of the sweet potato slices in the baking dish, then place the onion, cauliflower, and fish on top. Cover with the remaining sweet potato slices. Warm the spelt milk, 1 tablespoon (15 g) coconut oil, and bouillon cubes in a saucepan, stirring continuously. Pour this mixture over the casserole and bake for an hour, or until cooked through.

YIELD: 4 SERVINGS

Snacks

~

Make small things with great love.

I snack twice a day. Mid-morning I usually eat something sweet and in the afternoon, I tend to prefer something savory and salty. The snacks I make can be frozen or kept in the fridge, which is why I like to make a whole bunch at a time so I always have something on hand.

MINI PIZZAS

THESE ARE A *creative* SNACK, IF I DO SAY SO MYSELF. THEY'RE GREAT FOR *sharing* OR FOR *indulging* IN ALL BY YOURSELF. AND THE BEST PART IS THERE'S *no dough* INVOLVED.

PREPARATION
20 MINUTES

INGREDIENTS
··· 1 ZUCCHINI
··· 2 TABLESPOONS (30 ML) OLIVE OIL
··· BLACK OLIVES, PITTED
··· 8 MUSHROOMS
··· 5 SLICES ORGANIC, COOKED TURKEY BREAST
··· 5 TABLESPOONS (75 ML) TOMATO SAUCE (PAGE 134)
··· HIMALAYAN SALT AND BLACK PEPPER, TO TASTE
··· 1 TABLESPOON (11 G) MUSTARD

DIRECTIONS

Preheat the oven to 400°F (200°C). Slice the zucchini diagonally into 3 thick slices and then cut each slice horizontally into 3 pieces. Lay the zucchini slices on a baking sheet and drizzle with the olive oil. Finely chop the black olives and the mushrooms, and cut the turkey slices in half. Top each of the zucchini slices with equal amounts of the turkey, tomato sauce, olives, and mushrooms (in this order), and season with salt and pepper. Bake the mini pizzas for 7 to 10 minutes in the oven, then place them on a serving dish and top each with a bit of mustard. That's it!

YIELD: 9 MINI PIZZAS

OVEN-ROASTED PEPPERS

THESE ARE THE EASIEST *stuffed peppers* EVER! THEY'RE SUPER TASTY AND ONLY TAKE *ten minutes* TO MAKE. THEY'RE PERFECT TO *share* WITH GUESTS, BUT I ALSO MAKE THEM FOR LUNCH, OR AS AN *appetizer* OR A SIDE DISH.

PREPARATION
20 MINUTES

INGREDIENTS
··· 3 MINI BELL PEPPERS
··· 1 TABLESPOON (15 G) COCONUT OIL, MELTED
··· ⅔ CUP (150 G) HOMEMADE HUMMUS (PAGE 128)
··· A FEW FRESH CILANTRO LEAVES
··· SEA SALT AND BLACK PEPPER (OPTIONAL)

DIRECTIONS

Preheat the oven to 350°F (180°C). Slice the peppers in half lengthwise. Remove the seeds and the stems, and rinse with water. Place the pepper halves on a baking sheet and brush them with a bit of coconut oil. Fill the pepper halves with hummus and bake for about 10 minutes in the oven. In the meantime, finely chop the cilantro and sprinkle it over the peppers once they're done. Season with salt and pepper to taste.

YIELD: 3 TO 6 SERVINGS

SNACK COOKIES

THESE DELICIOUS, *guilt-free* COOKIES ARE PERFECT TO HAVE ON HAND TO ACCOMPANY A CUP OF *coffee* OR TEA, OR JUST TO EAT AS AN *afternoon snack*.

PREPARATION
40 MINUTES

INGREDIENTS
- 1 CUP (150 G) HAZELNUTS
- 1¼ CUPS (180 G) ALMONDS
- 1 CUP (130 G) SPELT FLOUR
- ¼ CUP (60 ML) WATER
- 6½ TABLESPOONS (100 ML) MAPLE SYRUP
- ¼ CUP (40 G) MEDJOOL DATES, PITTED
- 2 TABLESPOONS (12 G) CHIA SEEDS
- 1 TABLESPOON (8 G) HEMP SEEDS
- 4 TABLESPOONS (32 G) CACAO POWDER
- 2 TABLESPOONS (30 G) COCONUT OIL
- 1 TEASPOON SEA SALT

SUPPLIES
FOOD PROCESSOR

DIRECTIONS
Preheat the oven to 350°F (180°C). Blitz the nuts in a food processor for a minute or two until very finely ground. Then add the remaining ingredients and process again until a sticky dough is formed. Spoon a tablespoon (15 g) of dough into your hands and roll it into a ball. Place it on a baking sheet and press it flat so it becomes thin and round. Repeat until all the dough is used up. Put the baking sheet in the oven and bake for about 20 minutes, until the cookies firm up and begin to brown. Allow them to cool for a few minutes and enjoy!

YIELD: 10 COOKIES

Tip! These freeze well.

CHOCO-SNACKS

MAYBE I EAT THESE *chocolate balls* A LITTLE TOO OFTEN—THEY'RE JUST WAY TOO EASY TO MAKE AND ARE SO *addictive!* THEY'RE GREAT WITH A CUP OF COFFEE OR *tea* AFTER A NICE DINNER WITH FAMILY OR FRIENDS. SOMETIMES I'LL BRING A COUPLE ALONG AS A *surprise* FOR MY LITTLE NEPHEW WHEN I VISIT, OR AS A TREAT WHEN I'M MEETING SOME FRIENDS.

PREPARATION
25 MINUTES

INGREDIENTS
- 1¼ CUPS (200 G) DATES, PITTED
- 1¼ CUPS (170 G) RAW UNSALTED MIXED NUTS
- ¼ CUP (60 G) COCONUT OIL
- 2 TABLESPOONS (16 G) RAW CACAO POWDER
- 1 TABLESPOON (6 G) CHIA SEEDS
- DRIED COCONUT

SUPPLIES
BLENDER OR FOOD PROCESSOR

DIRECTIONS

Soak the dates in water to cover for 15 minutes. Pulverize the nuts, coconut oil, cacao powder, and chia seeds in a blender or food processor. Add the dates and blend once again. Spoon the mixture into a bowl and let stand for 10 minutes. Then, roll the mixture into small balls and coat with dried coconut. Chill the finished balls in the fridge for an hour and then they're ready to eat!

YIELD: 15 TO 20 BALLS

RAW SNACK BARS

THE KNOWLEDGE THAT I'VE GOT ONE OF THESE BARS IN MY *handbag* MAKES ME SUPER *happy*. THESE BARS ARE SWEET, FULL OF *healthy* INGREDIENTS, AND VERY *filling,* SO EATING JUST ONE GIVES ME THE ENERGY I NEED TO KEEP GOING. THIS RECIPE CALLS FOR A BUNCH OF INGREDIENTS, BUT IT YIELDS ABOUT *twenty* BARS THAT YOU CAN EAT OVER THE COURSE OF A WEEK OR TWO.

PREPARATION
85 MINUTES

INGREDIENTS
- 2½ CUPS (250 G) WALNUTS
- ¼ CUP (50 G) GROUND FLAXSEEDS
- 1/3 CUP PLUS 1 TABLESPOON (50 G) HEMP SEEDS
- ⅔ CUP (100 G) CACAO NIBS
- ½ CUP (50 G) GRATED COCONUT, PLUS MORE FOR SPRINKLING
- ⅔ CUP (100 G) SUNFLOWER SEEDS
- ⅔ CUP (100 G) CHIA SEEDS
- ⅔ CUP (75 G) DRIED WHITE MULBERRIES
- 2 TEASPOONS LUCUMA POWDER
- 3 TABLESPOONS (45 G) COCONUT OIL, MELTED
- 2 CUPS (350 G) DATES, PITTED
- 8 FIGS
- ⅔ CUP (100 G) RAISINS
- 3 TABLESPOONS (48 G) APPLE BUTTER

SUPPLIES
FOOD PROCESSOR, BAKING DISH
(8" X 8", OR 20 X 20 CM)

DIRECTIONS

Put three-quarters of the ingredients up to and including the lucuma powder in the food processor. Then add the coconut oil, dates, figs, raisins, and apple butter, and blitz until the mixture starts to stick to itself. Add a bit more coconut oil and dates if the mixture is too dry. Then add the remainder of the ingredients and process again. Spread the mixture evenly across the bottom of a shallow 8 x 8-inch (20 x 20 cm) dish. Sprinkle with grated coconut and place the dish in the fridge for at least an hour. Once cooled, cut into small bars.

YIELD: 20 BARS

Tip! Also delicious with bits of dark chocolate or a handful of blueberries added.

BANANA BREAD

THIS BREAD IS *too good*. HAVE IT FOR BREAKFAST (WITH JAM, IF YOU'D LIKE) OR AS A SNACK WITH A BIG MUG OF *tea*. IT'S SWEET AND *moist*, BUT HEALTHY AND *gluten free*.

PREPARATION
AHEAD OF TIME: 8 MINUTES
TOTAL TIME: 60 MINUTES

INGREDIENTS
- 1²⁄₃ CUPS (200 G) BUCKWHEAT FLOUR
- 2 TEASPOONS BAKING POWDER
- 1 TEASPOON GROUND CINNAMON
- ¼ CUP (60 G) UNSWEETENED APPLESAUCE
- 3 BANANAS, PUREED
- 1 TEASPOON PURE VANILLA EXTRACT
- 3 EGGS
- PINCH OF HIMALAYAN SALT OR SEA SALT
- 1 TABLESPOON (15 G) COCONUT OIL, MELTED

SUPPLIES
LOAF PAN (8" X 4", OR 20 X 10 CM)

DIRECTIONS

Preheat the oven to 350°F (180°C) and grease the loaf pan with coconut oil. Whisk all the ingredients together in a mixing bowl until combined. Pour the batter into the loaf pan and just bake! The bread will be done in 45 minutes and it's even more decadent after having spent a night or two in the fridge.

YIELD: 1 LOAF

OSAWA CAKE

THIS RECIPE IS A PERFECT ACCOMPANIMENT TO A CUP OF *coffee*. THE CAKE IS SWEET, FILLING, MOIST, AND FULL OF *nuts* AND DRIED *fruit*. IT'S BOTH REALLY TASTY AND REALLY *nutritious*. SINCE I DISCOVERED OSAWA CAKE, I MAKE IT ALL THE TIME. I'LL OFTEN EVEN EAT A THICK SLICE OF IT FOR BREAKFAST.

PREPARATION
80 MINUTES

INGREDIENTS
- 1 CUP (150 G) RAISINS
- 1 CUP (200 G) BROWN RICE
- 2 TABLESPOONS (30 G) COCONUT OIL
- ½ CUP (70 G) SESAME SEEDS, TOASTED
- 1 CUP (150 G) HAZELNUTS
- 1 CUP (125 G) SPELT FLOUR
- 6 DRIED APRICOTS OR FIGS, CHOPPED
- ¾ CUP (180 ML) ORGANIC FRUIT JUICE CONCENTRATE
- 1¼ CUPS (100 G) OATMEAL
- 1 TEASPOON PURE VANILLA EXTRACT
- 2½ TABLESPOONS (20 G) GROUND CINNAMON
- 1 TEASPOON SEA SALT

SUPPLIES
LOAF PAN (8" X 4", OR 20 X 10 CM)

DIRECTIONS

Soak the raisins in water for 20 minutes. Preheat the oven to 350°F (180°C). Rinse the rice and cook it fully according to package directions. In the meantime, grease the loaf pan with the coconut oil.

Use three-fourths of the sesame seeds to coat the bottom and sides of the pan. Roast the nuts briefly in a frying pan over high heat without any oil.

When the rice is cooked, mix it with the remainder of the ingredients until it forms a sticky batter (not too dry, but also not too wet). Transfer the batter to the loaf pan and press it down well. Sprinkle the top with the remaining sesame seeds. Bake the cake for 45 to 60 minutes. The cake will still be moist when it's done. Allow to cool completely and then enjoy!

YIELD: 12 SERVINGS

"For those of us with a real sweet tooth: heat 1 tablespoon (8 g) cacao powder, 1 tablespoon (15 g) coconut oil, and 1 tablespoon (15 ml) agave syrup in a saucepan, and add a couple handfuls of popcorn. Stir well to coat and then enjoy!"

POPCORN

Movie night? PARTY? OR JUST FEEL LIKE *noshing?* POPCORN IS THE *quickest* SNACK EVER. IT TAKES A MAXIMUM OF *five minutes* TO MAKE AND ONLY REQUIRES A POT WITH A TIGHT-FITTING LID.

PREPARATION
10 MINUTES

INGREDIENTS
··· ½ TABLESPOON COCONUT OIL
··· HANDFUL OF POPCORN KERNELS
··· SEA SALT OR HIMALAYAN SALT

DIRECTIONS
Melt the coconut oil in a pot with a tight-fitting lid. Rinse the popcorn kernels in a sieve. Transfer the kernels to the pot, close the lid, and cook for 2 to 3 minutes over high heat until the popping sound has stopped. Put the popcorn in a bowl and sprinkle with a bit of salt. Ready to eat!

YIELD: 1 SERVING

Inca berries hail from the high-elevation, tropical regions of South America. This exotic and delicious snack is not only a treat for your taste buds, but it's also just really good for you. Inca berries are sweet with a slightly sour aftertaste and are full of vitamins.

PRIMAL SNACKS

THIS SNACK IS MADE WITH PURE, *primal ingredients*. THIS PERFECT COMBINATION OF *dates*, NUTS, AND *coconut* MAKES FOR AN ADDICTIVE SNACK. THEY TASTE *sweet*, SOUR, AND *creamy*—IN SPITE OF THE FACT THAT THERE'S NO CREAM INVOLVED.

PREPARATION
10 MINUTES

INGREDIENTS
- ¾ CUP (120 G) ALMONDS
- ⅔ CUP (120 G) DATES, PITTED
- ¾ CUP (120 G) CASHEWS
- 1 CUP (150 G) DRIED INCA BERRIES
- 1 TABLESPOON (15 ML) NUT MILK
- GRATED COCONUT

SUPPLIES
FOOD PROCESSOR, IMMERSION BLENDER, OR BLENDER

DIRECTIONS

Blend the almonds, dates, cashews, Inca berries, and nut milk in a food processor or using an immersion blender. You can also use a regular blender. Once combined, roll the mixture into small balls and coat completely with grated coconut. They're juicy and delicious when eaten fresh!

YIELD: 8 BALLS

CHICKPEA SNACK

IF YOU *season* CHICKPEAS AND ROAST THEM IN THE OVEN UNTIL CRISPY, THEY MAKE A *surprisingly* TASTY SNACK. THEY'RE A *healthy* ALTERNATIVE TO CHIPS OR SALTED PEANUTS AND THEY'RE THE PERFECT SNACK FOR A PARTY.

PREPARATION
40 MINUTES

INGREDIENTS
··· 2 TABLESPOONS (30 G) COCONUT OIL
··· 1 CUP (230 G) COOKED CHICKPEAS
··· 1 TABLESPOON (7 G) PAPRIKA
··· 1 TEASPOON SALT
··· 1 TEASPOON BLACK PEPPER
··· PINCH OF CAYENNE
··· 1 TEASPOON THYME

DIRECTIONS

Preheat the oven to 400°F (200°C). Melt the coconut oil in a saucepan, add the remainder of the ingredients, and stir well to coat the chickpeas. Spread the chickpeas across a baking sheet or in an ovenproof dish and bake for 15 minutes. Give the chickpeas a stir at this point and then bake for another 10 minutes, until they're golden brown and crunchy.

YIELD: 4 SERVINGS

94

My ultimate temptation! An order of fries with a nice big dollop of mayonnaise is not particularly healthy, but I should actually eat it more often because it makes me so happy. Being the health freak that I am, I headed to the kitchen to make fries out of sweet potatoes and parsnips. And they're just as good! See page 132 for a healthier version of mayonnaise to go along with the fries.

Power
Food

PARSNIP FRIES

PREPARATION
20 MINUTES

INGREDIENTS
··· 3 PARSNIPS
··· 1 TABLESPOON (15 G) COCONUT
    OIL, MELTED
··· 2 TABLESPOONS (6 G) THYME
··· SEA SALT, TO TASTE

SUPPLIES
BAKING SHEET

DIRECTIONS
Preheat the oven to 400°F (200°C). Peel the parsnips, wash them, and slice them into thin strips. Place them on a baking sheet, drizzle with the coconut oil, and sprinkle with the thyme and a bit of salt. Toss to coat evenly. Bake for 30 minutes. They're tasty with a dollop of mayonnaise or another dip (see spreads).

YIELD: 2 SERVINGS

SWEET POTATO FRIES

PREPARATION
20 MINUTES

INGREDIENTS
··· 2 LARGE SWEET POTATOES
··· 4 TABLESPOONS (60 G)
    COCONUT OIL
··· 1 TEASPOON PAPRIKA
··· HIMALAYAN SALT, TO TASTE

DIRECTIONS
Wash the sweet potatoes. I don't peel them, but you can if you'd like. Slice them into long, thin fries. Heat the coconut oil in a pan over high heat. When the oil is hot, add the sweet potato fries, making sure you watch out for spattering oil. Remove the fries from the oil when they begin to brown. Place a sieve over a bowl and place the fries in the sieve to allow any excess oil to drain. You can always save the excess oil for the next time. Sprinkle the fries with the paprika and salt, give them a shake, transfer them to a nice bowl, and you're done! They're delicious with mixed nut butter or with my healthy mayonnaise (page 132).

YIELD: 2 SERVINGS

SWEET POTATOES

Sweet potatoes are not potatoes at all! Really. These "potatoes" are unrelated in terms of origin. Sweet potatoes have a sweet flavor and are full of vitamins A and C, calcium, magnesium, and potassium, and they contain at least one and a half times as many antioxidants as blueberries. They're filling too. I use sweet potatoes in soups and salads, and I even make fries out of them!

KALE CHIPS

FORGET KALE AND SAUSAGE; KALE CHIPS ARE *the new thing*. IN NEW YORK, YOU CAN GET THIS SNACK ON EVERY STREET CORNER, SO AS A *kale country*, IT'S OUR DUTY NOT TO BE LEFT BEHIND HERE. YOU CAN BUY THESE *healthy* CHIPS IN SPECIALTY STORES, BUT IT'S MUCH MORE FUN (AND VERY EASY) TO MAKE THEM YOURSELF. I'LL EAT A WHOLE *bowl* OF THESE WHILE WATCHING A GOOD *movie*.

PREPARATION
25 MINUTES

INGREDIENTS
··· 5 CUPS (300 G) KALE LEAVES
··· 1 TABLESPOON (15 ML) OLIVE OIL
··· 1 TEASPOON SOY SAUCE
··· 1 TEASPOON SESAME SEEDS

DIRECTIONS

Preheat the oven to 350°F (180°C). Remove the hard stalks from the kale leaves. Wash the leaves and allow them to dry. Then rip the leaves into large pieces and put them in a bowl. Add the oil, soy sauce, and sesame seeds. The leaves should glisten a bit, but be sure not to use too much oil. Taste and adjust the seasoning (soy sauce) if necessary. Toss the leaves thoroughly and lay them on a baking sheet. Bake the leaves for between 6 and 12 minutes, depending on your oven. Keep your eye on them and take them out of the oven when they turn nice and crispy.

YIELD: 4 SERVINGS

Power Food

Sweets

No sugar. I'm already sweet enough.

Of course it's best not to get too accustomed to a lot of sweetness in your diet. But because we develop a preference for this taste from the time we're young, we really can't do without it. I don't eat any refined sugar, but using natural sweeteners in cakes and snacks really does taste even better! Do be aware that even with natural sweeteners, you need to exercise some restraint—eat these only in moderation.

Ice cream every day! Why not? You can go nuts with these healthy ice-cold snacks.

POPSICLES

I MAKE THESE *popsicles* FOR MY SWEET LITTLE BUDDY—*my nephew*. HE LOVES THEM! BUT TO BE HONEST, MY FRIENDS AND I ALSO HAPPILY *devour* THESE ALL *summer* LONG.

PREPARATION
6 HOURS

INGREDIENTS
··· 1 MANGO
··· 4 KIWIS
··· SMALL TUB (ABOUT 8 OUNCES, OR 225 G) STRAWBERRIES
··· 3 TABLESPOONS (45 ML) WATER

SUPPLIES
6 POPSICLE MOLDS

DIRECTIONS

Wash the fruit, peel the kiwis, hull the strawberries, and chop into pieces. Puree each of the fruits and the berries separately using an immersion blender and add 1 tablespoon (15 ml) of the water to each fruit mixture to thin it out. Fill the popsicle molds one-third full with the first layer—mango. Place in the freezer for 1 to 2 hours. Repeat with the kiwi layer and then the strawberry layer. Insert the popsicle sticks into the last layer and place the popsicles in the freezer overnight. The next day you'll have 6 popsicles to share or to keep all to yourself. Short on time? Blend all the fruit together with the water until creamy. Pour into the popsicle molds and freeze for several hours.

YIELD: 6 POPSICLES

STRAWBERRIES

They look good enough to eat! Strawberries are a tasty, healthy snack for any moment of the day. When I was young, I used to pick them in our garden and eat them sliced on a rice cake with a bit of honey. It was so delicious! Strawberries are little vitamin C bombs, and they're great in fruit salads and smoothies, or as dessert.

PISTACHIO ICE CREAM

FORGET GELATO. THE *tastiest* PISTACHIO ICE CREAM IS THE ONE YOU MAKE *yourself*.

PREPARATION
25 MINUTES

INGREDIENTS
- 2 LARGE HANDFULS SHELLED PISTACHIOS, DIVIDED
- PINCH OF SEA SALT
- 1 TABLESPOON (15 ML) MAPLE SYRUP
- ½ AVOCADO
- 2 FROZEN RIPE BANANAS, SLICED
- 1 TEASPOON PURE VANILLA EXTRACT
- ½ TEASPOON ALMOND EXTRACT
- 1 TABLESPOON (15 ML) ALMOND MILK (OPTIONAL, PAGE 156)

SUPPLIES
FOOD PROCESSOR

DIRECTIONS

Roughly chop a handful of pistachios and toast them in a dry frying pan with a pinch of salt. Add the maple syrup, stir, and allow to cool. Add the avocado, frozen bananas, vanilla, almond extract, almond milk (if needed, depending on how thick the mixture is), and the remainder of the pistachio nuts to a food processor, and process until a creamy ice cream is formed. Don't over-process here! You're not looking to make a milkshake. Serve the ice cream in bowls, with a good sprinkling of the toasted nuts.

YIELD: 2 SERVINGS

Power Food

VANILLA-COCONUT ICE CREAM

YOU NEED AN *ice cream maker* TO MAKE THIS ICE CREAM. IT'S A BIG PURCHASE, BUT ONCE YOU TRY THIS RECIPE, YOU'LL BE *hooked* AND WILL SOON SEE HOW *worthwhile* HAVING AN ICE CREAM MACHINE CAN BE.

PREPARATION
AHEAD OF TIME: 5 HOURS
ACTIVE PREPARATION: 10 MINUTES

INGREDIENTS
- 2⅓ CUPS (350 G) CASHEWS
- 3 CUPS (250 G) COCONUT MEAT
- 1 CUP (240 ML) WATER
- 1 TABLESPOON (15 ML) PURE VANILLA EXTRACT
- 6 TABLESPOONS (90 ML) AGAVE SYRUP, OR TO TASTE
- PINCH OF SEA SALT

SUPPLIES
BLENDER, ICE CREAM MAKER

DIRECTIONS
Soak the cashews in water to cover for at least 4 hours in the fridge. Then puree all the ingredients in a blender on high speed. Put the mixture in the fridge for a couple of hours, then transfer to your ice cream maker and follow the manufacturer's instructions to transform the mixture into ice cream.

YIELD: 6 POPSICLES

Power Food

CHOCOLATE ICE CREAM

PURE *happiness!* THAT'S WHAT ANY CHOCOLATE ICE CREAM BRINGS ME, BUT *this one,* WITH ITS HEFTY DOSE OF *cacao powder,* HAS BECOME MY ULTIMATE *happy potion.*

PREPARATION
15 MINUTES

INGREDIENTS
··· 2 FROZEN BANANAS
··· 3 TABLESPOONS (45 G) NUT
    BUTTER (PAGE 127)
··· 3 TABLESPOONS (24 G)
    CACAO POWDER
··· 1 TABLESPOON (15 ML) AGAVE
    SYRUP (OPTIONAL)
··· SPLASH OF ALMOND MILK (PAGE 156)
··· RAW CHOCOLATE BITS, FOR
    GARNISH

SUPPLIES
BLENDER

DIRECTIONS
Add the frozen bananas, nut butter, cacao powder, and agave syrup
to a blender and blitz. If the mixture is too thick, add a splash of almond
milk. If the mixture sticks to the sides of the blender jar, scrape them
using a spatula. Serve the ice cream with raw chocolate bits sprinkled
over the top.

YIELD: 2 SERVINGS

RAW "OREOS"

WHEN I LIVED IN NEW YORK, I SAW EVERYONE DEVOURING THESE *cookies*. THEY ARE *divine*. BUT WHEN YOU LOOK AT THE PACKAGING, YOU KNOW YOU'RE NOT MAKING YOUR *body* VERY HAPPY BY EATING THEM. *Not to worry!* I FIGURED OUT A HEALTHY *version* OF THE COOKIES THAT WILL MAKE YOUR BODY *happy*.

PREPARATION
AHEAD OF TIME: 4 HOURS
ACTIVE PREPARATION: 30 MINUTES

INGREDIENTS
CASHEW CREAM
··· 1 CUP (130 G) RAW CASHEWS
··· 2 TEASPOONS WATER
··· 1 TEASPOON PURE VANILLA EXTRACT
··· 1 TABLESPOON (15 G) COCONUT OIL, MELTED
··· PINCH OF SALT
··· 1 TABLESPOON (15 ML) AGAVE SYRUP

COOKIES
··· 2/3 CUP (100 G) DATES, PITTED
··· 1/2 CUP (50 G) OATMEAL
··· 1¼ CUPS (180 G) ALMONDS
··· 1 CUP (120 G) RAW CACAO POWDER
··· 1/2 TEASPOON GROUND CINNAMON

SUPPLIES
BLENDER

DIRECTIONS

To make the cashew cream, soak the cashews in water to cover for 4 hours. Drain.

To make the cookies, soak the dates in water to cover for about 15 minutes. Drain. Add the cookie ingredients in the order they appear, bit by bit, to the blender. Blend well until the mixture is finely ground and forms a dough. Remove the dough from the blender, place it on a sheet of parchment paper, and roll it out using a rolling pin. Using a cookie cutter or the lid of a jar, cut the dough into small circles. Place the cookies on a plate and when you have cut all the cookies, put the plate in the fridge.

Wash out the blender, then fill with the ingredients for the cashew cream and mix until creamy. Transfer the cream to a small bowl. Remove the cookies from the fridge, spoon a teaspoon of the cashew cream onto a cookie, and top with another cookie so that the "sandwich" is formed. Repeat until there are no cookies remaining.

YIELD: 12 COOKIES

Tip! You need a nice, strong blender if you want finely ground nuts. If yours isn't tough enough, be sure to chop the nuts before putting them in the blender. Is the mixture sticking to the sides of the blender jar? Stop the blender every so often to scrape down the sides using a spatula.

CHEESECAKE

This cake has it all! IT'S MY FAVORITE WHEN I'M CRAVING SOMETHING TANGY, *savory*, AND SWEET. WHAT'S MORE, THIS CAKE LOOKS FANTASTIC TOO. IT REALLY STEALS THE *show*, ESPECIALLY WHEN YOU TELL YOUR GUESTS THAT THEY CAN ENJOY IT GUILT-FREE. IF THERE ARE LEFTOVERS, YOU CAN STORE THE CAKE IN THE *freezer* FOR THE NEXT *party*.

PREPARATION
AHEAD OF TIME: 1 HOUR
ACTIVE PREPARATION: 30 MINUTES

INGREDIENTS
FILLING
- 4 CUPS (600 G) RAW CASHEWS
- 1 CUP (240 G) COCONUT OIL, PLUS EXTRA FOR GREASING
- ⅔ CUP (160 ML) LEMON JUICE
- ¾ CUP (180 ML) AGAVE SYRUP
- ½ CUP (120 ML) WATER
- PINCH OF SEA SALT
- 2 TEASPOONS PURE VANILLA EXTRACT

CRUST
- 2 CUPS (300 G) ALMONDS
- 2 CUPS (300 G) DATES, PITTED

TOPPING
- 4 TABLESPOONS (60 G) CHERRY JAM, NO SUGAR ADDED

SUPPLIES
BLENDER, SPRINGFORM PAN
(10", OR 24 CM, IN DIAMETER)

DIRECTIONS

To make the filling, soak the raw cashews in water to cover for at least an hour. Drain.

Meanwhile, make the crust by pulverizing the almonds and dates in a blender until finely ground. Grease the springform pan with a bit of coconut oil and press the almond-date mixture into the bottom, covering the entire surface. Clean out the blender.

Combine the drained cashews with the other filling ingredients in the blender. Blend until creamy, then pour the filling over the crust. Put the cake in the freezer overnight and then thaw for about 3 hours in the fridge the next day. Spoon the cherry jam on top of the cake and it's ready to be served and enjoyed thoroughly!

YIELD: 12 SERVINGS

CHOCO-MUFFINS

THESE MUFFINS, MADE WITH *raw cacao*, BANANA, DATES, AND SPELT FLOUR, MAKE ME *so happy!* I'LL OFTEN BRING THEM WITH ME WHEN I'M GOING TO EAT AT A FRIEND'S PLACE, EITHER FOR *dessert* OR ALONGSIDE A CUP OF TEA. AND ONCE IN A BLUE MOON, I'LL WHIP SOME UP FOR MYSELF TO EAT AS A *snack.*

PREPARATION
45 MINUTES

INGREDIENTS
- ⅔ CUPS (200 G) SPELT FLOUR
- ½ CUP PLUS 2 TABLESPOONS (75 G) RAW CACAO POWDER
- ½ CUP PLUS 2 TABLESPOONS (120 G) COCONUT BLOSSOM SUGAR
- 1 TABLESPOON (8 G) BAKING POWDER
- ½ TEASPOON SEA SALT
- 1 TEASPOON PURE VANILLA EXTRACT
- 2 BANANAS
- 1 EGG
- 1 CUP (175 G) DATES, SOAKED AND PITTED
- 6 TABLESPOONS (90 G) COCONUT OIL
- 6½ TABLESPOONS (100 ML) WARM WATER

SUPPLIES
BLENDER, MUFFIN PAN, PAPER MUFFIN LINERS

DIRECTIONS

Preheat the oven to 350°F (180°C). Place liners in 8 cups of a muffin tin. Combine the spelt flour, cacao, coconut blossom sugar, baking powder, and sea salt in a large mixing bowl. Add the remaining ingredients to a blender and process until creamy. Pour the liquid mixture into the dry mixture and stir well to combine. Spoon 2 tablespoons (30 g) of batter into each of 8 muffin cups and bake for 35 minutes, until a toothpick inserted in the center comes out clean.

YIELD: 8 MUFFINS

"Love is sweet,
please take a treat."

FAMILY KROES' FAVORITE CUPCAKES

TO PERFECT THESE CUPCAKES, I LOCKED MYSELF UP FOR *days* IN MY *MEM*'S KITCHEN IN *Eastermar*. AFTER SOME TRIAL AND ERROR, THIS RECIPE WAS OFFICIALLY *approved* BY THE MOST CRITICAL JURY EVER: MY FAMILY. NOW, WHEN I GO TO THE NORTH WITH THESE CUPCAKES IN TOW, I CAN BARELY MAKE IT INTO THE HOUSE BEFORE THEY DISAPPEAR. *Success* IS GUARANTEED!

PREPARATION
90 MINUTES

INGREDIENTS
BOTTOM LAYER
- ⅓ CUP (50 G) ALMONDS
- ½ CUP (60 G) PECANS
- 1 CUP (170 G) DATES, PITTED
- PINCH OF SEA SALT

MIDDLE LAYER
- ½ CUP (120 G) MIXED NUT BUTTER (PAGE 127)
- 1 CUP (170 G) DATES, PITTED
- ¼ CUP (50 G) COCONUT OIL
- PINCH OF SALT
- PINCH OF UNSWEETENED VANILLA POWDER

TOP LAYER
- ⅓ CUP (70 G) COCONUT OIL
- 4 TABLESPOONS (20 G) CACAO POWDER
- ¼ CUP (90 G) AGAVE SYRUP OR PALM SUGAR

SUPPLIES
BLENDER, MUFFIN PAN, PAPER MUFFIN LINERS

DIRECTIONS

Place liners in 10 cups of a muffin tin. To make the bottom layer, mix the ingredients in the blender until finely ground. Press the mixture down evenly into the muffin cups. Be sure to press firmly. Rinse the blender.

To make the middle layer, mix the ingredients in the blender until finely ground. This time, the texture will be a bit softer. Spoon the paste on top of the bottom layer in the muffin cups.

To make the top layer, warm the coconut oil in a small saucepan, add the cacao powder and agave syrup, and stir well. This layer is the softest. Pour this mixture on top of the previous two layers, coating them fully. Freeze the cupcakes for about an hour and then dive in!

YIELD: 10 CUPCAKES

PHYLLON'S BIRTHDAY CAKE

I MADE THIS CAKE FOR MY NEPHEW *Phyllon's* BIRTHDAY. IT HAS SINCE BECOME A BIT OF A *tradition* THAT I, HIS PROUD *auntie,* BAKE HIM A (SECRETLY HEALTHY) CAKE EACH YEAR. AT LEAST A MONTH IN ADVANCE OF HIS BIRTHDAY, HE'LL ALREADY HAVE CAKE ON THE BRAIN. THERE'S NO REFINED SUGAR IN THIS *chocolate cake,* BUT IT IS STILL NICE AND SWEET. IT'S BEEN APPROVED BY MY NEPHEW, SO IT'S DEFINITELY *kid-proof!*

PREPARATION
30 MINUTES

INGREDIENTS
CRUST
- 1⅓ CUPS (200 G) WALNUTS
- 2¼ CUPS (400 G) DATES, PITTED
- 1 CUP (125 G) RAW CACAO POWDER
- 1 TEASPOON PURE VANILLA EXTRACT
- PINCH OF SEA SALT

FILLING
- 1 CUP (225 G) COCONUT BUTTER*
- 2 CUPS (250 G) RAW CACAO POWDER
- 4 CHUNKS (75 G) CACAO BUTTER
- 2 TABLESPOONS (30 G) COCONUT OIL
- SMALL HANDFUL OF CHERRIES, PITTED
- ⅞ CUP (200 ML) MAPLE SYRUP
- 1 TEASPOON PURE VANILLA EXTRACT
- 1 TEASPOON SEA SALT
- 1 TABLESPOON (5 G) GRATED COCONUT
- SMALL HANDFUL OF RAW MIXED NUTS

SUPPLIES
BLENDER, SPRINGFORM PAN
(8", OR 20 CM, IN DIAMETER)

DIRECTIONS

To make the crust, process the walnuts and dates, little by little, in a blender. Add the raw cacao powder, vanilla, and sea salt and blend to combine. Remove the mixture from the blender and knead using your hands for 2 minutes. Place the nut dough on the bottom of the springform pan and press down firmly so that the bottom is covered.

To make the filling, combine the coconut butter, cacao powder, cacao butter, coconut oil, cherries, maple syrup, vanilla, and sea salt in the blender, and process until thick and creamy. Pour the mixture on top of the crust and use a spatula to spread it evenly. Decorate the filling with the grated coconut and nuts. Chill the cake in the fridge for an hour and then it's ready to enjoy.

*HOW DO YOU MAKE COCONUT BUTTER? PROCESS 1 POUND (450 G) GRATED COCONUT IN THE BLENDER UNTIL IT BECOMES CREAMY. THAT'S IT! YOU CAN ALSO ADD A BIT OF HONEY AND VANILLA TO IT FOR A SWEETER, WARMER FLAVOR.

YIELD: 20 SERVINGS

SUPER(FOOD) ICE CREAM CAKE

SUPERFOOD = SUPER *good!* AND THAT APPLIES COMPLETELY TO THIS *fantastic* ICE CREAM CAKE. MAKE IT FOR DESSERT AT A GARDEN BARBECUE OR AS A BIRTHDAY CAKE FOR A PARTY AT THE *park.* FEEL FREE TO EAT AN EXTRA-LARGE PIECE OF THIS CAKE—IT'S *super healthy!*

PREPARATION
12 HOURS

INGREDIENTS

BOTTOM LAYER
- 1 CUP (150 G) CASHEWS, DIVIDED
- 4¹⁄₃ CUPS (650 G) ALMONDS, DIVIDED
- ¹⁄₃ CUP (50 G) BRAZIL NUTS
- 1 TEASPOON PURE VANILLA EXTRACT OR UNSWEETENED VANILLA POWDER
- 1 TABLESPOON (15 G) COCONUT OIL
- 10 DATES, PITTED

MIDDLE LAYER
- ¹⁄₃ CUP (50 G) CASHEWS
- 2 CUPS (300 G) ALMONDS
- 5 TABLESPOONS (75 ML) MAPLE SYRUP
- 6 DATES, PITTED
- 1¹⁄₂ FROZEN BANANAS
- 1 TEASPOON GROUND CINNAMON
- 1 TEASPOON PURE VANILLA EXTRACT OR UNSWEETENED VANILLA POWDER
- 2 TEASPOONS MACA POWDER
- 2 TABLESPOONS (10 G) CHIA SEEDS
- 1 TABLESPOON (15 ML) COCONUT MILK

TOP LAYER
- ¹⁄₃ CUP (50 G) CASHEWS
- ³⁄₄ CUP (125 G) BLUEBERRIES
- ¹⁄₃ CUP (50 G) CHERRIES, PITTED
- 2¹⁄₂ CUPS (250 G) FROZEN CRANBERRIES
- 1¹⁄₂ FROZEN BANANAS
- 1²⁄₃ CUPS (250 G) STRAWBERRIES, STEMS REMOVED
- 1 TABLESPOON (8 G) CAMU CAMU POWDER
- 2 TEASPOONS (10 ML) COCONUT MILK
- 4 DATES, PITTED

DIRECTIONS

To prepare, soak ²⁄₃ cup (100 g) of the cashews and 2 cups (300 g) of the almonds in water to cover for at least 4 hours. Do the same for the cashews and almonds for the middle and top layers. Drain.

To make the bottom layer, combine the nuts, vanilla powder, coconut oil, and dates in a blender, and process until finely ground. Remove the mixture from the blender, and knead for a few minutes by hand. Then press the mixture into the bottom of the springform pan, covering it entirely. Rinse out the blender.

To make the middle layer, process all the ingredients in the blender until creamy. Pour this mixture into the springform pan and place it in the freezer for 30 minutes. Rinse the blender again with warm water.

To make the top layer, add all the ingredients to the blender and process until a nice, thick, pink mixture is formed. You can also use other types of fruit for this layer, such as blackberries and red currants. After 30 minutes in the freezer, remove the cake and pour the last layer on top. Chill in the freezer for about 6 hours. Remove the cake from the freezer. Wow! You can decorate the cake with fresh fruit or nuts.

SUPPLIES
BLENDER, SPRINGFORM PAN (10", OR 25 CM, IN DIAMETER)

YIELD: 10 SERVINGS

Spreads

~

Complaining won't burn calories.

~

The cherry on top! A dip or delicious topping can often make a dish. All of these spreads are great on a cracker or a slice of bread. They're all nutritious and guilt-free.

CHOCOLATE SPREAD

I *treat* MYSELF FROM TIME TO TIME WITH THIS *sweet* SPREAD ON A CRACKER AFTER LUNCH. IT'S ALSO TASTY ON A *pancake.* AS A TEENAGER, I WENT TO PARIS QUITE A BIT AND ON EVERY STREET CORNER THERE YOU'D FIND EXACTLY THAT COMBINATION. FULL OF SUGAR, OF COURSE, AND AFTER A *crêpe* LIKE THAT I'D LITERALLY BE BOUNCING DOWN THE STREETS OF THE FASHION CAPITAL. WHEN YOU MAKE CHOCOLATE SPREAD *yourself,* WITHOUT SUGAR, YOU CAN INDULGE WITHOUT FEELING *guilty.* THIS PARTICULAR VARIANT IS EVEN GOOD FOR YOU!

PREPARATION
20 MINUTES

INGREDIENTS
··· 1 CUP (135 G) HAZELNUTS
··· ¼ CUP (30 G) RAW CACAO POWDER
··· 1 TABLESPOON (15 G) COCONUT OIL
··· 1 TABLESPOON (15 ML) HAZELNUT OIL
··· 5 TABLESPOONS (75 ML) AGAVE SYRUP
··· 1 TABLESPOON (15 ML) VANILLA EXTRACT
··· PINCH OF SEA SALT

SUPPLIES
FOOD PROCESSOR

DIRECTIONS

Preheat the oven to 350°F (180°C). Spread the hazelnuts on a baking sheet and roast in the oven for 8 to 10 minutes, until they begin to darken. Peel the hazelnuts by wrapping them in a clean tea towel and rubbing the skins off. Grind the nuts in the food processor for about 7 minutes, until a smooth butter is formed. Then add the cacao powder, coconut oil, hazelnut oil, agave syrup, vanilla, and salt, and mix again until smooth. If the mixture is on the dry side, you can add a bit more oil. Store the spread in a glass container and bring it to room temperature about a half an hour before you plan to eat it. It's delicious on spelt bread, a rice cake, a crunchy cracker, or in desserts.

YIELD: 200 G, ABOUT 10 SERVINGS

NUT BUTTER

My favorite spread! I LOVE THIS ON A *rice cake* WITH SLICED *avocado*. I ALSO USE NUT BUTTER AS A *topping* FOR OATMEAL OR COOKIES. AND SOMETIMES I CAN'T RESIST JUST DIPPING MY *finger* DIRECTLY IN THE JAR.

PREPARATION
20 MINUTES

INGREDIENTS
- 1 CUP (150 G) ALMONDS
- 1 CUP (150 G) HAZELNUTS
- PINCH OF SEA SALT

SUPPLIES
FOOD PROCESSOR

DIRECTIONS

Preheat the oven to 350°F (180°C). Spread the almonds and hazelnuts on a baking sheet, sprinkle with sea salt, and roast in the oven for 8 to 10 minutes, until they begin to brown. Remove the nuts from the oven and allow them to cool. Transfer the nuts to the food processor and blend until finely ground. It takes 5 to 10 minutes to process the nuts and you'll see them go through different stages—they'll change from being coarsely ground to forming a fine meal, and then the oils in the nuts will begin to be released. You need to keep blending until the nuts liquefy and the mixture becomes creamy. Add a bit more sea salt to taste and spoon the nut butter into a small glass jar. The nut butter will keep for quite a while, but I don't know how long it'll last—not long in my kitchen, in any case!

YIELD: 300 G, ABOUT 10 SERVINGS

HOMEMADE HUMMUS

I EAT *so much* HUMMUS. I PUT IT ON RICE CAKES, ADD IT ON THE SIDE OF *salads,* OR DIP CELERY STICKS INTO IT AS A SNACK. YOU CAN BUY HUMMUS AT THE GROCERY STORE, BUT THE TASTIEST, HEALTHIEST, AND BEST HUMMUS IS THE ONE YOU MAKE YOURSELF. IT'S *very easy* TO DO!

PREPARATION
15 MINUTES

INGREDIENTS
- 2 CLOVES GARLIC
- 1 TABLESPOON (15 G) TAHINI (PAGE 143)
- 3 TABLESPOONS PLUS 1 TEASPOON (50 ML) FRESHLY SQUEEZED LEMON JUICE
- 4 TABLESPOONS (60 ML) FILTERED WATER
- 1¼ CUPS (300 G) CANNED CHICKPEAS, RINSED AND DRAINED
- 1 TEASPOON GROUND CUMIN
- 1 TABLESPOON (15 ML) OLIVE OIL, PLUS MORE FOR SERVING
- PINCH OF CAYENNE, PLUS MORE FOR SERVING
- 1 TEASPOON SALT

SUPPLIES
BLENDER

DIRECTIONS
Mince the garlic and combine it with the tahini, lemon juice, and water in the blender and mix until smooth. Then add the chickpeas, cumin, olive oil, and cayenne. Process again, adding water if needed. Sprinkle the mixture with sea salt and blend for another minute, until it becomes soft. Serve in a bowl, drizzled with olive oil and sprinkled with a bit more cayenne.

YIELD: 4 SERVINGS

This jam will keep for at least a week in an airtight container in the fridge.

CHIA JAM

THIS IS A *sweet jam*, FREE OF REFINED SUGAR, WITH AN EXTRA *boost* FROM CHIA SEEDS. EVERY SO OFTEN, I'LL MAKE A JAR THAT I'LL UNDOUBTEDLY EAT WITHIN A WEEK. IT'S TASTY ON A CRACKER, BUT IT'S ALSO GREAT IN *oatmeal* OR AS A TOPPING FOR *muffins* OR A CAKE.

PREPARATION
30 MINUTES

INGREDIENTS
··· 2 CUPS (300 G) FRESH BLUEBERRIES
··· 3 TABLESPOONS (45 ML) MAPLE SYRUP, OR TO TASTE
··· 2½ TABLESPOONS (12 G) CHIA SEEDS
··· 1 TEASPOON PURE VANILLA EXTRACT

DIRECTIONS
Bring the blueberries and the maple syrup to a boil in a saucepan over high heat. Lower the heat and simmer for 5 minutes, stirring frequently. Puree the blueberries using a potato masher or a fork and then stir in the chia seeds. Continue simmering for another 15 minutes over low heat, stirring often. Remove from the heat once the mixture begins to thicken and add the vanilla. If you think it needs more sweetness, you can add a bit more maple syrup.

YIELD: 300 G, ABOUT 10 SERVINGS

Tip! Mash the basil leaves with a pestle for a more intense basil flavor.

PESTO

I ALWAYS HAVE A *basil plant* GROWING IN MY KITCHEN AND I OFTEN CATCH MYSELF BRUISING A LEAF WITH MY FINGERS, JUST TO SMELL IT. AMAZING! THIS PESTO SMELLS JUST AS GOOD AND TASTES *even better*. THE NICE THING ABOUT *homemade* PESTO IS THAT YOU KNOW EXACTLY WHAT GOES INTO IT AND WHAT DOESN'T. I EAT PESTO ON CRUNCHY CRACKERS, AS A DIP, OR AS THE *finishing touch* ON A TASTY PASTA DISH. *Delizioso!*

PREPARATION
10 MINUTES

INGREDIENTS
··· 2 CLOVES GARLIC
··· ⅓ CUP (45 G) PINE NUTS
··· 1 SHALLOT
··· 1½ CUPS (60 G) BASIL LEAVES
··· ½ CUP (50 G) FRESHLY GRATED
    HARD GOAT'S MILK CHEESE
··· 7 TABLESPOONS (100 ML) EXTRA
    VIRGIN OLIVE OIL
··· 2½ TABLESPOONS (10 G) CHOPPED
    PARSLEY

SUPPLIES
BLENDER OR FOOD PROCESSOR

DIRECTIONS
Finely grind all the ingredients in the blender or food processor.

YIELD: 250 G, ABOUT 4 SERVINGS

MAYONNAISE

IT MIGHT NOT BE THE *healthiest* RECIPE IN THIS BOOK, BUT HOMEMADE MAYO IS ALWAYS TASTIER AND *better for you* THAN THE KIND YOU BUY AT THE STORE. IT DOES TAKE A BIT OF PATIENCE TO MAKE MAYONNAISE, AND EVERY TIME YOU MAKE IT, THERE'S SOME UNCERTAINTY AS TO WHETHER OR NOT IT WILL ACHIEVE THE *right consistency*. MY FATHER USED TO MAKE IT HIMSELF AT HOME AND IT WASN'T ALWAYS A SURE THING. AFTER LOTS OF TRIAL AND ERROR, I BELIEVE THIS TO BE THE *ultimate* RECIPE.

PREPARATION
20 MINUTES

INGREDIENTS
- 3 CLOVES GARLIC
- 2 EGG YOLKS
- 1 TABLESPOON (15 ML) LEMON JUICE
- 1 TEASPOON POWDERED GINGER
- 1 TEASPOON MUSTARD
- SEA SALT AND PEPPER, TO TASTE
- PINCH OF DRIED PARSLEY
- 7/8 CUP (200 ML) RICE OIL

SUPPLIES
MORTAR AND PESTLE, IMMERSION BLENDER

DIRECTIONS
Finely mash the garlic using the mortar and pestle, and place it in a large, glass liquid measuring cup. Add the remaining ingredients with the exception of the oil. Place the immersion blender in the cup and, while the blender is running, begin to slowly drizzle oil into the cup until the mixture thickens. Once that happens, you can add oil a bit more quickly until it has all been added. Season with salt and pepper, if needed. Use the mayo right away or store it in the fridge.

YIELD: 180 G, ABOUT 12 SERVINGS

TOMATO SAUCE

MAKE YOUR OWN *classic* TOMATO SAUCE. IT'S MUCH *healthier* THAN PREMADE SAUCE AND YOU CAN TASTE IT! YOU CAN *spice up* THE SAUCE AS MUCH AS YOU WANT. IT'S DELICIOUS OVER PASTA WITH A BIT OF GOAT CHEESE AND *basil,* AND MEAT EATERS CAN ADD *ground beef* OR *chicken* AS WELL.

PREPARATION
70 MINUTES

INGREDIENTS
- 3⅓ POUNDS (1½ KG) RIPE ROMA TOMATOES
- 1 ONION
- 3 CLOVES GARLIC
- 1 TABLESPOON EXTRA VIRGIN OLIVE OIL
- 1 TEASPOON OREGANO
- 1 TEASPOON YELLOW SAMBAL (OPTIONAL, PAGE 142)
- SEA SALT AND BLACK PEPPER, TO TASTE
- A FEW BASIL LEAVES, FINELY CHOPPED (OPTIONAL)

DIRECTIONS
Chop the tomatoes, onion, and garlic into small pieces. Add the olive oil to a medium-size pan and sauté the onion for 2 minutes over medium-high heat. Then add the garlic, oregano, tomatoes, and sambal. Let the sauce simmer for about 30 minutes. Stir often using a wooden spoon to prevent the sauce from sticking. Once the sauce has thickened up, press it through a sieve or vegetable mill. Return the strained sauce to the pan and simmer over low heat for another 30 minutes. Season with salt and pepper to taste, and sprinkle with finely chopped basil.

YIELD: 4 SERVINGS

SNACK SAUCE

I MAKE SURE TO ALWAYS HAVE A JAR OF THIS IN MY *fridge.* I *dip* (HOMEMADE) FRIES IN IT, AND *celery* AND CARROT STICKS TOO. *So good!*

PREPARATION
4 HOURS

INGREDIENTS
··· 1¼ CUPS (180 G) CASHEWS
··· 1 TABLESPOON (15 ML) WATER
··· 1 TEASPOON LEMON JUICE
··· 3 TABLESPOONS (45 ML) ALMOND
    MILK (PAGE 156)
··· PINCH OF SEA SALT

SUPPLIES
BLENDER

DIRECTIONS

Soak the cashews in water for at least 4 hours. Drain the nuts and transfer to the blender. Add the remaining ingredients and process until creamy. Yum!

YIELD: 200 G, ABOUT 20 SERVINGS

GUACAMOLE

THIS ONE IS A BIG *hit!* I MAKE THIS *avocado dip* FOR PARTIES, TO GO WITH DRINKS, OR FOR A BARBECUE WITH FRIENDS. THE ONLY DOWNSIDE IS THAT THE BOWL IS USUALLY EMPTY WITHIN MINUTES . . . *Everybody loves it!* IT'S ALSO GREAT ON A CRUNCHY *cracker* OR RICE CAKE FOR *lunch* OR A SNACK.

PREPARATION
15 MINUTES

INGREDIENTS
- 4 RIPE AVOCADOS
- 1 CLOVE GARLIC
- ½ RED ONION
- 3 SPRIGS FRESH CILANTRO
- 8 CHERRY TOMATOES
- 2 TABLESPOONS (30 ML) EXTRA VIRGIN OLIVE OIL
- SEA SALT OR HIMALAYAN SALT AND BLACK PEPPER, TO TASTE
- LIME JUICE (OPTIONAL)

SUPPLIES
BLENDER

DIRECTIONS

Halve the avocados, remove the pits, and spoon the flesh into the blender. Finely chop the garlic, onion, cilantro, and tomatoes. Add the garlic and half the chopped onion to the blender with the avocados. Blend until creamy. Transfer the mixture to a bowl, and add the remaining onion and the cilantro, tomatoes, oil, salt, and pepper. Stir well to combine. Sprinkle with lime juice to prevent browning.

YIELD: 4 TO 8 SERVINGS

AVOCADO

One of my favorite fruits! Avocado is healthy and delicious. Think avocados are unhealthy because of their high fat content? No way! They are rich in good, healthy fats. Even if you're watching your weight you can still enjoy avocados. What's more, they are full of fiber, which is filling and helps calm your hunger. They are delicious in salads and smoothies, or just mashed on crackers.

SID'S DIP

THIS RECIPE WAS CREATED BY NONE OTHER THAN . . . MY *love*. I WAS COMPLETELY TAKEN BY *surprise* WHEN HE HANDED ME A CRACKER TOPPED WITH THIS DIP. AS I'M SURE YOU CAN *imagine,* I'M THE ONE THAT DECIDES WHAT'S FOR DINNER, BUT I HAVE TO GIVE IT TO HIM—*the man can cook!* WE USUALLY EAT THIS *fish dip* AS A SNACK, BUT WE ALSO EAT IT ON *rice cakes* FOR LUNCH.

∽

PREPARATION
15 MINUTES

INGREDIENTS
- 6 OUNCES (150 G) SMOKED MACKEREL
- 2 CLOVES GARLIC
- 1 RED ONION
- ⅔ CUP (150 ML) TOMATO SAUCE (PAGE 134)
- ½ VEGETABLE BOUILLON CUBE
- 1 TEASPOON OREGANO
- 2 PINCHES OF CAYENNE
- BLACK PEPPER, TO TASTE

SUPPLIES
BLENDER

DIRECTIONS
Slice the mackerel in half and remove the bones. Add the mackerel to the blender along with the garlic and red onion. Blend until smooth. Transfer the mixture to a pan and combine with the tomato sauce. Warm the dip over low heat and crumble the half bouillon cube over the top. Stir well until the mixture thickens, remove from the heat, and allow it to cool. Season the dip with the oregano, cayenne, and black pepper.

YIELD: 300 G, ABOUT 30 SERVINGS

YELLOW SAMBAL

Ooh la la . . . THIS SAMBAL IS *hot!* IT'S EASY TO MAKE IT YOURSELF AND IT'S MUCH HEALTHIER WITHOUT ALL THE ADDITIVES, SUGAR, AND ARTIFICIAL FLAVORING. EATING SPICY FOOD FROM TIME TO TIME IS GOOD FOR YOUR BODY AND *mind.* IT LITERALLY *spices things up.* I ADD A BIT OF THIS SAMBAL TO THE HOMEMADE HUMMUS ON A CRUNCHY CRACKER AND MIX IT INTO MY PASTA SALADS OR *saoto soup* JUST TO KEEP THINGS *interesting.*

PREPARATION
15 MINUTES

INGREDIENTS
··· 20 LARGE, YELLOW MADAME
    JEANETTE CHILE PEPPERS
··· 2 LARGE CLOVES GARLIC
··· 1 SMALL ONION
··· 1 TABLESPOON (11 G) MUSTARD
··· 4 TABLESPOONS (60 ML)
    SESAME OIL
··· 1 TABLESPOON (15 ML) LEMON
    JUICE

SUPPLIES
BLENDER

DIRECTIONS
Add the chile peppers, garlic, onion, and mustard to a blender. While the machine is running, add the sesame oil, bit by bit. Add the lemon juice and blend again until a thick paste is formed.

YIELD: 4 SERVINGS

Store the tahini in an airtight glass container in the fridge. It will keep for months.

TAHINI

I'VE BEEN EATING TAHINI SINCE I WAS *two* YEARS OLD. I USED TO MAKE *little cakes* WITH IT, ON RICE CAKES WITH HONEY AND *wheat germ*. THESE DAYS I'LL EAT IT AS A SNACK OR WITH LUNCH. YOU CAN BUY SESAME SEED PASTE IN MOST GROCERY STORES, BUT *making it yourself* IS EASY AND IT REALLY DOES *taste better*.

PREPARATION
30 MINUTES

INGREDIENTS
··· 1 POUND (450 G) SESAME SEEDS
··· SEA SALT

SUPPLIES
BLENDER OR FOOD PROCESSOR

DIRECTIONS

Bring out the flavor of the sesame seeds by roasting them. Preheat the oven to 350°F (180°C) and spread the seeds on a baking sheet. Once the oven is at the correct temperature, roast the seeds for 10 to 15 minutes, stirring occasionally to ensure that none of the seeds burns. Remove from the oven and allow the seeds to cool. Once cool, combine them with sea salt in a blender and process for 5 to 10 minutes, until the tahini is smooth and creamy. Then it's ready to eat!

YIELD: 450 G, ABOUT 30 SERVINGS

Drinks

Chase nothing but drinks and dreams.

Every day, I enjoy fresh juices, smoothies, and hot drinks—they're actually the foundation of my healthy lifestyle. I enjoy them for breakfast, as snacks, and as an energy shot. Sometimes I'll bike to a juice bar, but I prefer to make them myself. Just chop up the ingredients, put them in the blender, and voilà!

SMOOTHIES

THOSE OF YOU WHO FOLLOW ME ON *social media* KNOW THAT I'M CRAZY ABOUT *juices* AND SMOOTHIES. I CAN'T EMPHASIZE ENOUGH HOW *easy* IT IS TO TAKE GOOD CARE OF YOUR BODY. YOU CHOP UP THE INGREDIENTS, THROW THEM IN THE BLENDER . . . *et voilà!* YOU CAN CHANGE THINGS UP *endlessly*, SO YOU NEVER HAVE TO DRINK THE SAME THING. NEED *inspiration?* THESE ARE MY FAVORITE SMOOTHIES, AND WITH AN *extra* INGREDIENT OR TWO, YOU'LL HAVE A *superboost!*

INGREDIENTS YIELD: 1 SMOOTHIE (ABOUT 2 CUPS, OR 500 ML)

Maroon Booster
- 1 PEAR
- 1 APPLE
- 1½ CUPS (45 G) SPINACH
- ⅔ CUP (100 G) BLUEBERRIES
- JUICE OF 1 LEMON
- JUICE OF 1 ORANGE
- ½ FROZEN BANANA
SUPERBOOST:
- 1 TEASPOON (8 G) WHEATGRASS POWDER

Detox
- 1 BANANA
- 1 PEAR
- 2½ TABLESPOONS (10 G) CHOPPED PARSLEY
- 1 TEASPOON POWDERED GINGER
- 1 CUP (240 ML) COCONUT WATER
SUPERBOOST:
- 1 TEASPOON CHLORELLA POWDER

Sunshine
- ⅔ MANGO
- JUICE OF 2 ORANGES
- JUICE OF 1 LIME
- 1 TABLESPOON (15 G) COCONUT OIL
- 5 TABLESPOONS (100 ML) ALMOND MILK (PAGE 156)
- 1 TEASPOON HONEY
SUPERBOOST:
- 1 TEASPOON GUARANA POWDER

Summer Breeze
- ½ MANGO
- ½ AVOCADO
- 5 STRAWBERRIES
- 1 BANANA

- 1 CUP (240 ML) COCONUT WATER
SUPERBOOST:
- 1 TEASPOON MACA POWDER

Mean Green
- JUICE OF 1 LIME
- JUICE OF 1 ORANGE
- ½ CUP (15 G) WATERCRESS
- ⅓ CUP (20 G) KALE
- ½ APPLE
- ½ HANDFUL FRESH MINT LEAVES
- 2 TABLESPOONS (30 ML) ELDERBERRY JUICE
- ½ PEAR
- ⅔ CUP (160 ML) UNSWEETENED RICE MILK
SUPERBOOST:
- 1 TEASPOON MACA POWDER

Skinny Green
- JUICE OF ½ LEMON
- ½ SPEAR PINEAPPLE
- 1 AVOCADO
- 2 CUPS (120 G) ICEBERG LETTUCE
- PINCH OF GINGER POWDER
- ¾ CUP (200 ML) COCONUT WATER
SUPERBOOST:
- 1 TABLESPOON (8 G) WHEATGRASS

Coffee Blast
- ½ CUP (120 ML) ORGANIC COFFEE
- 5 TABLESPOONS (100 ML) ALMOND MILK (PAGE 156)
- 1 TABLESPOON (5 G) RAW CACAO POWDER
- 1 TABLESPOON (16 G) NUT BUTTER (PAGE 127)

- 1 BANANA
- 1 TEASPOON AGAVE SYRUP (OPTIONAL)

Hemp Smoothie
- ¾ CUP (180 ML) HEMP MILK (PAGE 157)
- 1 BANANA
- 1 APPLE
- ½ CUP (80 G) FROZEN BLUEBERRIES
- 2 TABLESPOONS (30 ML) ELDERBERRY JUICE
- 1 TEASPOON GROUND CINNAMON
- 1 TABLESPOON (20 G) HONEY OR COCONUT BLOSSOM NECTAR
SUPERBOOST:
- 1 TEASPOON CAMU CAMU POWDER

Orange on Top
- 1 BANANA
- ⅔ CUP (160 ML) ALMOND MILK (PAGE 156)
- 1 TEASPOON GROUND CINNAMON
- 1 TABLESPOON (15 G) COCONUT OIL
- 1 TEASPOON TURMERIC
- ¼ CUP (25 G) GOJI BERRIES
- PINCH OF GROUND BLACK PEPPER

Sourberry Power
- 1 CUP (150 G) FROZEN BLUEBERRIES, STRAWBERRIES, OR RASPBERRIES
- ⅓ CUP (75 ML) CRANBERRY JUICE
- ¾ CUP (180 ML) RICE MILK
- 5 TABLESPOONS (100 ML) COCONUT MILK
- 1 TABLESPOON (7 G) GROUND FLAXSEEDS
SUPERBOOST:
- 1 TEASPOON LUCUMA POWDER
- 1 TABLESPOON (5 G) RAW PROTEIN POWDER

SUPPLIES
BLENDER

DIRECTIONS

Simply mix all of the ingredients in the blender until a tasty, fresh smoothie is formed and enjoy!

Coffee Blast

CITRUS FRUIT

Citrus fruits aren't only beautiful when you slice them open, but they're also very good for you. The various kinds of citrus fruits—such as lemons, limes, mandarins, and grapefruit—help you keep your vitamin C levels in check. They are a great way to start the day and a great way to quench your thirst.

FEEL-GOOD DRINK

A COUPLE OF TIMES A WEEK, I END MY DAY WITH THIS FEEL-GOOD DRINK. IT RELAXES ME. GINGER HAS A WARMING EFFECT, *chamomile* CALMS YOUR BODY, AND *lemon* AND *turmeric* AID *digestion*. AFTER DRINKING THIS, I *sleep* WELL AND MY *skin* GETS A BOOST. I WAKE UP THE NEXT DAY WITH MORE ENERGY THAN I HAD THE DAY BEFORE!

PREPARATION
5 MINUTES

INGREDIENTS
··· 1 TEASPOON TURMERIC
··· PINCH OF POWDERED GINGER
··· 1 TEASPOON HONEY
··· 1 CHAMOMILE TEABAG
··· PINCH OF GROUND BLACK PEPPER
··· JUICE OF ½ LEMON

DIRECTIONS
Put all of the ingredients in a large mug or heatproof glass and pour boiling water over the top. Let steep, then remove the teabag.

YIELD: 1 LARGE GLASS OR MUG

Tip! Use the leftover mango for a smoothie—combine it with kale, apple, lemon juice, grapefruit juice, and a bit of water. Delicious!

ICED TEA

THIS IS A DELICIOUS, COOLING, THIRST-QUENCHING *summer drink*. SERVE IT IN A *cocktail glass* WITH AN UMBRELLA AND *you're ready to enjoy the sun!*

PREPARATION
15 MINUTES

INGREDIENTS
··· 2 MANGOES
··· ½ CUP (120 ML) COLD GREEN TEA
··· ⅔ CUP (160 ML) COCONUT MILK
··· 1 TABLESPOON (20 G) HONEY

SUPPLIES
JUICER, BLENDER

DIRECTIONS
Peel the mangoes and remove the stones. Process them in the juicer. Add the mango juice and the remaining ingredients to the blender and mix until smooth.

YIELD: 2 CUPS (480 ML)

HOT ENERGY DRINK

THIS DRINK MAKES YOU *happy* AND POWERFUL, AND GIVES YOU *instant energy!* LIKE LIME AND *mint,* CAYENNE PEPPER IS GOOD FOR MOVING THE BOWELS, AND FOR YOUR SKIN AND YOUR *immune system.* IT ALSO GIVES YOU AN ENERGY BOOST. *Cinnamon* MAKES THIS TEA NICE AND SPICY, REGULATES YOUR BLOOD SUGAR, AND IS A POWERFUL *antioxidant.* HONEY HELPS FIGHT *infection* AND MAKES THIS DRINK NICE AND SWEET.

PREPARATION
5 MINUTES

INGREDIENTS
··· ½ LIME
··· 1 CUP (240 ML) BOILING WATER
··· PINCH OF GROUND CINNAMON
··· PINCH OF CAYENNE
··· 1 TEASPOON HONEY
··· SMALL HANDFUL OF MINT LEAVES

DIRECTIONS
Squeeze the half lime into a mug and add the boiling water. Add the rest of the ingredients with the exception of the mint and stir well. Then add the mint and let the drink steep for 3 minutes. A delicious afternoon boost!

YIELD: 1 SERVING

HAZELNUT MILK

I USE HAZELNUT MILK TO MAKE *cookies* AND OTHER *sweets*. IT'S ALSO DELICIOUS *blended* INTO SMOOTHIES.

PREPARATION
3½ HOURS

INGREDIENTS
- ⋯ 2 CUPS (250 G) HAZELNUTS
- ⋯ 3 DATES, PITTED
- ⋯ 1 QUART (1 L) FILTERED WATER
- ⋯ ½ TEASPOON PURE VANILLA EXTRACT
- ⋯ PINCH OF SEA SALT

SUPPLIES
BLENDER, CHEESECLOTH OR A FINE SIEVE

DIRECTIONS
Soak the nuts and dates in water to cover for about 3 hours. Drain. Then combine all the ingredients in the blender and process on the highest speed setting. Pour the contents through a cheesecloth or sieve and collect the hazelnut milk in a bowl underneath. Squeeze the cheesecloth or press the liquid out using a spoon if you're using a sieve. Pour the milk into a bottle to store or use it right away in another recipe.

YIELD: 1 QUART (1 L)

IN MY RECIPES, I USE NUT MILK, RICE MILK, HEMP MILK, OR COCONUT MILK. USUALLY I'LL JUST BUY A PACK AT MY LOCAL ORGANIC FOOD STORE, BUT YOU CAN ACTUALLY JUST MAKE IT YOURSELF. IT'S REALLY NOT DIFFICULT AT ALL! AND THE PLUS IS THAT YOU CAN MAKE AS MUCH OR AS LITTLE AS YOU NEED. YOU CAN ALSO MAKE THE MILK TO SUIT YOUR OWN TASTES BY ADDING MORE OR LESS SWEETENER OR ADDING SPICES. HOMEMADE MILK WILL KEEP IN THE FRIDGE FOR FOUR TO FIVE DAYS IN AN AIRTIGHT CONTAINER. IF YOU'VE MADE TOO MUCH, JUST FREEZE IT. MY FAVORITE IS CREAMY NUT MILK.

Tip! Don't throw the leftover almond pulp away! Incorporate it into a cake or homemade bread.

ALMOND MILK

I USE THIS ALMOND MILK TO MAKE PORRIDGE IN THE *morning*, OR I'LL *heat* IT UP TO ADD TO MY *coffee*.

PREPARATION
AT LEAST 8½ HOURS

INGREDIENTS
- 1⅔ CUPS (250 G) RAW SWEET ALMONDS
- 1 QUART (1 L) FILTERED WATER
- PINCH OF SEA SALT
- ½ TEASPOON PURE VANILLA EXTRACT
- 1 TABLESPOON (15 ML) AGAVE SYRUP OR (20 G) HONEY (OPTIONAL)

SUPPLIES
BLENDER, CHEESECLOTH OR FINE SIEVE

DIRECTIONS

Soak the almonds in water to cover for 8 to 12 hours. Drain the almonds and add them to the blender along with the filtered water, sea salt, vanilla, and agave syrup, and process for a minute or two. Grab a bowl and spread the cheesecloth over the top. If you're using a sieve, place it on top of the bowl. Pour the almond mixture through the cheesecloth or sieve, ensuring that you squeeze out as much of the liquid as possible. There you go! Now you've got yourself some truly delicious almond milk!

YIELD: 1 QUART (1 L)

OAT MILK

I love oats. THEY'RE SORT OF *boring,* BUT THEY ARE VERY GOOD FOR YOU. THAT'S WHY I USE THEM FOR JUST ABOUT EVERYTHING . . . EVEN MILK!

PREPARATION
30 MINUTES

INGREDIENTS
- ½ CUP (50 G) OATMEAL
- 3¼ CUPS (750 ML) FILTERED WATER
- 1 TABLESPOON (15 ML) ALMOND OIL (OPTIONAL)
- 1 TEASPOON PURE VANILLA EXTRACT OR UNSWEETENED VANILLA POWDER
- PINCH OF HIMALAYAN SALT
- A COUPLE DROPS OF STEVIA (OPTIONAL)

SUPPLIES
BLENDER, CHEESECLOTH OR FINE SIEVE

DIRECTIONS

Soak the oats in water to cover for 20 minutes. Drain the oats using a sieve, and blend the oats and filtered water in a blender. Pour through a cheesecloth or sieve, collecting the oat milk in a bowl underneath. Squeeze the cheesecloth, or press the liquid out using a spoon if you're using a sieve. Transfer the strained milk back into the blender, add the remaining ingredients, and process until well combined. Pour the oat milk into a nice jug or bottle and enjoy!

YIELD: 3 CUPS (710 ML)

HEMP MILK

HEMP SEEDS ARE A *fantastic* SUPERFOOD. THEY'RE GOOD FOR YOUR MUSCLES, BONES, AND *teeth,* AND FOR *detoxifying* YOUR BODY. YOU CAN MAKE A NICE CREAMY MILK OUT OF THEM TOO. *Super easy.* AND NO, IT WON'T GET YOU *high.*

PREPARATION
10 MINUTES

INGREDIENTS
- 2 CUPS (250 G) PEELED HEMP SEEDS
- 2½ CUPS (600 ML) FILTERED WATER
- 3 DATES, PITTED
- 1 TEASPOON PURE VANILLA EXTRACT OR UNSWEETENED VANILLA POWDER

SUPPLIES
BLENDER

DIRECTIONS

Put the hemp seeds in the blender. Add the water, dates, and vanilla. Blend for a few minutes until a creamy, smooth milk is formed. *Et voilà*! Just like with all the other types of milk, store the hemp milk in a bottle. Use or drink it just as you would cow's milk.

YIELD: 1 QUART (1 L)

"Green."

JUICES

I MAKE A BIG GLASS OF JUICE FOR MYSELF AT LEAST THREE OR FOUR TIMES A WEEK. IT'S A GOOD WAY TO INCORPORATE *superfoods* INTO MY DIET. AND ONCE IN A WHILE, I'LL PLAN A JUICE DAY TO CLEANSE MY BODY. A DAY LIKE THAT MAKES YOU FEEL *fit* AND *clean*. THE BEST THING TO DO IS CONSULT WITH A *nutritionist* TO DISCUSS WHAT KIND OF JUICE DETOX WOULD BE BEST FOR YOU. IN TERMS OF JUICING, CENTRIFUGAL JUICERS DO THE JOB, BUT YOU SHOULD REALLY INVEST IN A *slow juicer*. JUICING WITH A SLOW JUICER PRESERVES MORE *flavor* AND *nutrients* FROM THE FRUITS AND VEGETABLES THAT YOU PROCESS.

SUPPLIES
BLENDER, SLOW JUICER OR CENTRIFUGAL JUICER

YIELD: 1²/₃ CUPS (400 ML)

Green
INGREDIENTS
- 1 LEMON
- 6 KALE LEAVES
- ½ CUCUMBER
- 1½ TABLESPOONS (6 G) FRESH PARSLEY
- 1 APPLE
- 1 SPEAR PINEAPPLE

DIRECTIONS
Peel the lemon and chop all the ingredients into small pieces. Process everything in the juicer. Easy does it!

Spicy
INGREDIENTS
- ¾ CUCUMBER
- 1 APPLE
- ½-INCH (1 CM) PIECE GINGER, PEELED
- 2 STALKS CELERY
- 1 BANANA
- HANDFUL OF MINT

DIRECTIONS
Process all of the ingredients, except the banana, in the juicer. Pour the juice into the blender, add the banana, and blend. You have a delicious, spicy juice.

Pink
INGREDIENTS
- 1½ CUPS (220 G) STRAWBERRIES, STEMS REMOVED
- ½ CUP (75 G) DICED WATERMELON
- 1 ORANGE, PEELED
- 1 LIME, PEELED

DIRECTIONS
You can juice the fruit to produce a true juice, without pulp. But you can also just toss everything in the blender. Just be sure to juice the orange and lime separately. It's more like a smoothie this way, but it's just as tasty.

Yellow
INGREDIENTS
- ½ LEMON
- 1 SPEAR PINEAPPLE
- ⅓ CUP (40 G) CHOPPED FENNEL
- ½-INCH (1 CM) PIECE GINGER, PEELED
- ¾ CUP (200 ML) COCONUT WATER
- 1 TABLESPOON (20 G) HONEY
- 1 TEASPOON TURMERIC
- ½ TEASPOON GROUND CINNAMON

DIRECTIONS
Peel the lemon. Chop the lemon and pineapple into small pieces and process the lemon, pineapple, fennel, and ginger in the juicer. Pour the juice into the blender, add the remaining ingredients, and blend.

Red
INGREDIENTS
- 1 APPLE
- 4 SMALL CARROTS
- 1 LARGE BEET
- 1 LIME, PEELED
- ½-INCH (1 CM) PIECE GINGER, PEELED
- SMALL HANDFUL OF MINT
- 3 TABLESPOONS (50 ML) ELDERBERRY JUICE

DIRECTIONS
Chop the apple, carrots, beet, lime, and ginger into small pieces and process in the juicer. Pour the juice into the blender, add the mint and elderberry juice, blend, and it's juice time!

GOJI BERRY SHAKE

GOJI BERRIES HAVE A *tangy-sour,* CHERRY-CRANBERRY FLAVOR. THE *berries* CONTAIN MORE THAN TWENTY MINERALS (1) AND AT LEAST EIGHTEEN *amino acids.* THEY'RE ALSO KNOWN FOR THEIR ABILITY TO *slow* THE BODY'S *aging process.* AND SO THIS SHAKE IS NOT ONLY *super tasty* AND REFRESHING, BUT IT ALSO GIVES YOUR BODY A SERIOUS *boost!* I MAKE THIS SHAKE QUITE OFTEN WHEN I FEEL AN AFTERNOON DIP COMING ON OR AS A *power breakfast.*

PREPARATION
3 HOURS AND 10 MINUTES

INGREDIENTS
··· 3 TABLESPOONS (30 G) GOJI
    BERRIES
··· ¾ CUP (200 ML) COCONUT WATER
··· 1 BANANA
··· LARGE HANDFUL OF FROZEN
    MIXED BERRIES
··· 1 TEASPOON FLAXSEEDS
··· 1 TEASPOON CHIA SEEDS

SUPPLIES
BLENDER

DIRECTIONS

Place the goji berries in a dish and add the coconut water. Let them soak overnight or for at least 3 hours. Add the contents of the dish to the blender, along with the banana, frozen berries, flaxseeds, and chia seeds. Blend to make a delicious shake.

YIELD: 1 SERVING

"One fresh juice a day keeps the doctor away."

Daily Schedules

NO TWO DAYS ARE EXACTLY THE *same*. THE THINGS I EAT AND DRINK ON A GIVEN DAY *depend* NOT ONLY ON WHAT I FEEL LIKE EATING BUT ALSO ON A *careful* ASSESSMENT OF WHAT I WILL BE DOING THAT DAY. BELOW ARE MY IDEAL *meal plans* FOR A *sporty* DAY, A *busy* DAY, AND A *lazy* DAY.

Sporty Day

7:00 a.m.   **Breakfast Quinoa** (page 20)
8:00 a.m.   **Workout**
9:30 a.m.   **Hemp Smoothie** (page 146)
12:00 p.m. **Rainbow Salad** (page 36)
3:00 p.m.   **Raw Snack Bar** (page 86)
6:00 p.m.   **Casserole** (page 75)

Busy Day

7:30 a.m.   **Warm water with the juice of 1/2 lemon**
8:00 a.m.   **Kick-Start Breakfast** (page 17)
10:30 a.m. **Choco-Snack** (page 83)
1:00 p.m.   **Quinoa Sushi with Green Juice** (pages 32, 159)
3:30 p.m.   **Kale Chips** (page 98)
6:30 p.m.   **Zucchetti "Pasta"** (page 68)
8:00 p.m.   **Feel-Good Drink** (page 151)

Lazy Day

9:00 a.m.   **Sweet Pancakes** (page 24)
12:00 p.m. **Choco-Muffin with Chocolate Spread on top** (pages 113, 124)
1:30 p.m.   **Slice of Osawa Cake** (page 89)
3:30 p.m.   **Raw "Oreos"** (page 111)
6:00 p.m.   **Pasta with Salmon** (page 70)
7:30 p.m.   **Vanilla-Coconut Ice Cream** (page 108)

My power food ingredients, their active properties, and other interesting facts.

Agave Syrup

Agave syrup is derived from the agave plant, which is a type of cactus. It's very sweet, but has a lower glycemic index than sugar. This means that it doesn't cause as sharp a spike in blood sugar as refined sugar does. It contains no vitamins or minerals, so use it in moderation.

Almonds

Almonds are high in fiber, which is good for digestion. They also contain a great deal of vitamin B, which is good for the heart and the brain. They're a source of vitamin E, which is great for the skin. I use both whole almonds and almond flour (ground almonds).

Amaranth

Amaranth contains iron, calcium, magnesium, vitamins B and E, phosphorus, and zinc. It's good for your bones and muscles.

Arugula

Arugula is a diuretic, promotes appetite, aids digestion, and has a painkilling effect.

Avocado

Avocados are a good source of protein, and they're high in vitamins C and E, carotenoids, selenium, zinc, and omega-3 fatty acids. They're great for the eyes and the skin, and help prevent and reduce inflammation. That they make you fat is simply untrue! Avocados contain good fats that give you energy.

Baking Powder

This is a healthy alternative to yeast that ensures that baked goods rise.

Bananas

It is a myth that bananas slow down digestive processes. On the contrary, they contain a great deal of fiber and good fats. Thanks to the potassium they contain, bananas contribute to achieving the correct balance of fluids in the body. They deliver energy quickly and can help cure a hangover because they contain magnesium. Bananas bind baked goods and make dishes creamy. And I just like them!

Basil

Basil contains lots of vitamins A and K, as well as minerals such as potassium, manganese, copper, and magnesium. It's good for eyesight, and helps fight colds and nausea. Due to the iron it contains, this plant is a good choice for those trying to fend off anemia.

Beets

Beets are nutritious, filled with essential vitamins and minerals, and aid in digestion. They have a positive effect on the kidneys and, last but not least, they detoxify and purify the body.

Black Pepper

The most important active substance in pepper is piperine. This encourages the production of stomach acid, and gallbladder and digestive enzymes, which all aid digestion. Eating pepper on a regular basis helps your body absorb vitamin B_{12}, beta-carotene, and selenium more efficiently from your food.

Buckwheat

Buckwheat is gluten-free and is a high-satiety food. It aids the immune system and improves muscle function.

Cacao (Raw)

Cacao is a natural source of magnesium, which is good for the bones, muscles, and teeth. Raw cacao relaxes muscles and helps combat stress. It also helps improve your mood because it increases serotonin production, so there's no limit to the chocolate you can eat!

Camu Camu

Camu camu, a fruit, is full of vitamin C. It supports the brain, eyes, heart, liver, lungs, skin, and the immune system. It staves off infection and promotes strong tendons and ligaments.

Carrot

Carrots are high in vitamins B_1, B_2, and C, and this combination accelerates wound healing. They strengthen the immune system and help you become and remain healthy. The beta-carotene they contain is good for your eyes.

Cauliflower

A wintertime source of vitamin C, which aids immunity, cauliflower contributes to liver detoxification.

Cayenne Pepper

Cayenne promotes good bowel function, is good for your skin and immune system, and gives you an energy boost. I sprinkle some in my Hot Energy Drink (page 153) and use it often in my cooking.

Celery

What multifaceted stalks! Celery helps stimulate appetite and is a diuretic. It alleviates kidney and bladder ailments, and reduces fever. It also stimulates metabolism. Suffering from gas? Celery can help! It can also help with arthritis and gout. It improves mood as well and helps fight bad breath, which is handy for those of us who love garlic!

Chamomile

Feel a headache or a migraine coming on? Have a cup of chamomile tea right away. It calms the nervous system and helps relieve menstrual pain. It's also good for fighting colds and flu, nausea, depression, muscle stiffness, allergies, sleeplessness, lower back pain, symptoms of menopause, and boils. Chamomile is a natural anti-inflammatory, painkiller, and disinfectant.

Chia Seeds

Chia seeds are full of omega-3 fatty acids, protein, and iron, and are a high-satiety food due to the relatively large amount of fiber they contain. Chia is a good replacement for dairy in your diet because it's a source of calcium, and the mineral boron (which, in turn, increases calcium absorption in the body). Healthy!

Chickpeas

This round legume is a low-calorie, high-satiety food. It keeps the blood sugar in balance and is high in minerals, fiber, and protein. It is also high in manganese, copper, iron, and phosphorus, as well as tryptophan, which is an essential amino acid that your body cannot produce on its own—it is only available via food sources. Tryptophan is required to produce serotonin in the body. There is evidence that serotonin improves mood and promotes sleep.

Chlorella

Chlorella is a natural detoxifier that aids in the removal of heavy metals such as mercury, lead, nickel, and aluminum, which are absorbed via your food and the air. Are you tired? Take chlorella—it will make you feel more fit in a flash, and it makes you stronger and healthier. I add these algae to my smoothies in powder form.

Cilantro

This tasty herb is high in iron. It is good for your blood, curbs the growth of bacteria, and increases metabolism. I use it in Asian dishes and in salads.

Cinnamon

This spice stabilizes blood sugar. It has a warming effect and helps relieve stomach cramps. I love it in my Hot Energy Drink (page 157) and think it's a tasty addition to my oatmeal!

Coconut Blossom Sugar

This sugar is unrefined and therefore still contains the nutrients that are required for your body to digest and process the sugar properly. It tastes a bit like caramel. I really like it for baking or making desserts.

Coconut Oil and Water

Coconut is a source of both saturated and unsaturated fats that are easily absorbed by the body and converted into energy. It helps prevent significant dips in blood sugar. I add a decent amount of coconut water or coconut oil to most of my smoothies. Super healthy! Coconut water is also a diuretic. I use coconut oil for frying and sautéing. It stands up to high heat without diminishing its nutritional value. I also use coconut oil outside of the kitchen—it keeps my skin and hair wonderfully soft.

Cranberries

These berries are tiny vitamin C bombs that are also high in fiber and antioxidants. They're great if you suffer from urinary tract infections because they help prevent bacteria from colonizing the urinary tract. They are also good for your heart, blood vessels, and teeth, and help combat stomach ulcers.

Cucumber

This vegetable is high in both water and fiber. It also contains vitamin C, silica, potassium, and magnesium. Cucumber juice is hydrating and keeps the skin healthy, smooth, and glowing.

Dried Fruit

Dried fruit is high in naturally occurring sugars and is therefore an ingredient that adds quite a bit of sweetness. It is also high in fiber, so it helps with producing bowel movements and aids digestion. I like to add dried apricots, figs, and dates to my muesli and granola. Nutrients like vitamin B, folic acid, iron, and potassium are retained in the drying process.

Eggs

Eggs are a fantastic meat replacement! They're full of omega-3 fatty acids, which are good fats. They are high in protein and vitamin B_{12}, and they are good for encouraging shiny hair and strong nails.

Elderberry

Elderberries are rich in tannins, amino acids, carotenoids, bioflavonoids, and rutin, as well as vitamins A, B, and C. The berries are well known for their antiviral properties and immune-supporting function. They help combat the flu, colds, stomach pain, and respiratory conditions.

Fennel

Fennel helps alleviate cramps and gas (even in babies and children), and stimulates milk production in lactating mothers. It helps with upset stomach, nausea, and, if used as a mouth rinse, it can fight inflammation of the gums. It has a positive effect on metabolism and therefore helps with weight loss. It works as a diuretic as well.

Fish

Fish, in particular wild fish, is protein-rich and high in healthy fats, omega-3s in particular. It also contains vitamins A, B, and D and iodine. Fish can have an antidepressant effect and is good for your brain. It also helps maintain a healthy weight.

Flaxseeds

Flaxseeds are high in fiber, which makes them excellent for the functioning of your intestines. They also contain omega-3 and omega-6 fatty acids, as well as vitamins B_1 and B_2, calcium, magnesium, and zinc. They are good for your eyes, skin, and hormonal balance.

Garlic

Garlic purifies the airways and the blood. It also activates the gastric juices and cleanses the intestinal tract. Raw garlic improves vitality and the functioning of organs like your adrenal glands, pancreas, liver, and spleen. Trying to avoid garlic breath? Be sure to combine your garlic with parsley.

Ginger

Ginger is a diuretic and an antipyretic. It also helps fight symptoms of colds and coughs. It is high in magnesium and phosphorus.

Goji Berries

These berries are high in vitamins B_1, B_2, B_3, B_6, C, and E, as well as minerals and essential fatty acids. They help slow the body's aging process and keep blood sugar and cholesterol in balance. They're delicious sprinkled over my Sweet Pancakes (page 24), added to a smoothie, or just as a snack on their own.

Hemp Seeds

Hemp seeds are relatively high in plant-based protein, which helps build muscle and increases endurance. They contain many minerals, such as magnesium, potassium, calcium, iron, zinc, copper, sulfur, and boron. These seeds are the perfect food for athletes—make yourself a Hemp Smoothie (page 146) after an intense workout to replace the protein you used up.

Honey

Honey has been used for centuries as an antidote to a wide variety of ailments, including colds, sore throats, compromised immunity, allergies, infections, stomach issues, anemia, and stiff joints. I always add it to my Feel-Good Drink (page 151). Truly delicious!

Inca Berries

These berries contain vitamins A, B_1, B_2, B_3, and C, as well as calcium, iron, and phosphorus. Due to their relatively high protein content, they are the perfect addition to a protein smoothie. Protein helps build muscle and aids in recovery, which is great after an intense workout. Inca berries are also a natural anti-inflammatory. They help combat free radicals and stall the aging process.

Kale

Kale contains high concentrations of healing nutrients such as vitamins A, C, and K as well as manganese. This combination of vitamins is great for bones, teeth, and the immune system. Kale also helps keep blood sugar stable. The iron it contains is good for the liver, and vitamin K helps fight inflammation. I use kale in stews, mashes, and smoothies, and to make chips (page 98).

Laos Powder

This superfood helps fight inflammation, calms the stomach, and stimulates metabolism. I think it's tasty and like to add it to soups and Asian dishes.

Lemon

Lemons are high in vitamin C and have a cleansing effect on the liver and, as a result, on the skin too. They also improve digestion in the stomach. Every morning, I drink a glass of lukewarm water with freshly squeezed lemon juice—it's a detoxifying way to start the day.

Lentils

Lentils are great for encouraging bowel movements. They are high in fiber and are a good source of energy. They are also high in plant-based protein and contain trace elements like iron, phosphorus, magnesium, and B vitamins.

Lucuma Powder

Lucuma is a delicious, sweet fruit that is made into a powder. I throw it in smoothies and shakes to add a bit of sweetness. It's also high in vitamins and minerals. Delicious!

Maca

Maca stabilizes blood pressure and blood sugar, and brings your hormones into balance. It encourages the healthy production of hormones and is therefore an aphrodisiac and can improve fertility.

Madame Jeanette Chiles

This chile pepper helps prevent a host of ailments due to its high vitamin and mineral content. Eating hot peppers and/or sambal each day helps prevent upper respiratory tract infections. Peppers keep the airways open and have an antimicrobial effect. These peppers are high in vitamin C and also contain a lesser amount of vitamins A, B_1, B_2, B_3, and B_6. I use these chile peppers to make my Yellow Sambal (page 142) and like to add a little bit to soup. Madame Jeanette peppers are fairly spicy!

Maple Syrup

This is the thickened sap of the maple tree. It contains a great deal of sucrose, very little fructose, and a host of vitamins and minerals like iron, calcium, and vitamin B_2.

Mint

Mint can soothe an upset stomach, increase metabolism, and give you energy. A cup of mint tea can give me a real boost!

Mulberries

Mulberries contain vitamins A, B_6, C, E, and K, and the minerals potassium, sodium, magnesium, selenium, iron, zinc, copper, and phosphorus. I use them in smoothies and eat them with breakfast or as a snack. Mulberries have a positive effect on the heart and blood vessels.

Nuts

Nuts are high in healthy fats and help keep your cholesterol in balance. They also contain iron, protein, calcium, and B vitamins. I use them a lot in my recipes, and tend to like walnuts, almonds, hazelnuts, and cashews.

Oats/Oatmeal

Oats contain unsaturated fats, vitamin B, calcium, and other minerals. They are good for your bones and help keep hunger at bay!

Parsley

This herb is full of nutrients like vitamins A, B, C, and K, as well as minerals like iron and potassium. It also contains chlorophyll, a substance that has strong antibacterial properties. That's why it's so effective at combating bad breath. Parsley can also help relieve stomach cramps and gas, and help bring on menstruation.

Parsnip

This root vegetable is high in vitamins B, C, and E, as well as iron, potassium, and calcium. The essential oils that parsnips contain help alleviate stomach and intestinal issues. They are rich in fiber and therefore help stabilize blood sugar. Parsnips are sweet-tasting but low in calories and saturated fats. They stimulate the kidneys and help the body rid itself of waste products. They are particularly good if you suffer from rheumatic ailments. Parsnips are also high in antioxidants and help combat free radicals.

Peas

Peas are rich in fiber, starch, protein, and B vitamins. They also contain iron, which can help combat fatigue and improve concentration. Peas decrease the risk of infection too.

Portobello Mushrooms

These mushrooms are high in protein and dietary fiber, which means they are a high-satiety food. They are also high in minerals like potassium phosphorus, copper, calcium, sodium, iron, and manganese, and vitamins B_1, B_2, B_6, and C, as well as folic acid. In need of a tasty appetizer? Try my Stuffed Portobello Mushrooms (page 57)!

Pumpkin

Pumpkin and squash are high in vitamin A and beta-carotene, and are therefore good for your eyes and skin. Pumpkin seeds are also very healthy because they contain vitamin E, magnesium, and selenium. Magnesium helps boost your energy. Pumpkin and squash are also high in fiber and protein. I often incorporate them into risotto, soups, and casseroles.

Quinoa

This seed is gluten-free and is perfect for vegetarians seeking plant-based protein. The combination of vitamins and minerals quinoa contains provides your body with an energy boost. I think it's a delicious base for many dishes. I sometimes even eat if for breakfast, but my very favorite way to eat quinoa is in my fresh Quinoa Salad (page 50).

Rosemary

This herb helps relieve cramped muscles, kills bacteria, and stalls viruses.

Samphire (Sea Beans)

Samphire is high in minerals like sodium, calcium, magnesium, and iodine. More and more people in Western society are becoming deficient in iodine.

Sea Salt

Salt is made up of sodium and chloride, and contains many other trace elements and minerals like magnesium, iodine (especially in Celtic sea salt), and bromine. Salt is a natural disinfectant and has a cleansing effect.

Seaweed

Seaweed is good for the proper functioning of the thyroid. The iron and protein content of seaweed makes it a particularly good choice for strict vegetarians and vegans. The calcium it contains is also good for your muscles and bones. It is high in vitamins A, B, and C, as well as iodine, magnesium, zinc, and fiber.

Sesame Seeds

Sesame seeds are high in protein. They have anti-inflammatory properties, protect the liver, and help keep blood sugar stable. I often sprinkle a spoonful of sesame seeds over a salad and I also incorporate them into my Osawa Cake (page 89).

Spelt

The best and oldest grain, spelt is much more easily digested by your body than wheat, for example. Spelt helps you stay regular and keeps blood sugar stabilized more effectively than wheat does.

Spinach

Raw spinach is high in chlorophyll, which helps cleanse the intestines. Chlorophyll is generally found in leafy, dark-green vegetables like spinach, parsley, and kale. It is good for your skin and is high in iron, which helps combat fatigue and dizziness. Spinach is also high in folic acid, which helps protect your cells, and beta-carotene, which is good for your eyes.

Stevia

Stevia is a good sugar substitute. As a kid, we always used to have a stevia plant growing in the garden. I used to pluck a couple of leaves and chew them for a while. Delicious! It's also a healthy addition to the dishes you make because the herb contains vitamins A and C, as well as minerals like calcium, magnesium, and zinc, among others. It contains no sugar or carbohydrates. These days, you can buy stevia in liquid form. Be aware! There are different versions of stevia on the market. Make sure you buy 100 percent pure stevia extract that doesn't contain any other additives.

Sunflower Seeds

These seeds are rich in magnesium and are good for your bones. In combination with calcium, this mineral helps balance the nervous system. Calcium and magnesium are a good combination for promoting relaxation and good sleep.

Sweet Potato

Sweet potatoes are high in vitamins A, B_6, and C, beta-carotene, iron, potassium, and calcium. Vitamin A and beta-carotene are good for your skin. These vitamins in combination with vitamin C make sweet potatoes effective at combating free radicals, which can contribute to premature aging.

Tea (Green)

Green tea stimulates your metabolism and fat-burning by your liver. It aids the immune system and also strengthens the cartilage in your joints. Green tea makes you more alert, better able to concentrate, and creative.

Tomato

Rich in vitamin C, zinc, calcium, and iron, tomatoes also contain lycopene, a powerful antioxidant. The redder the tomato, the more lycopene it contains. Tomatoes stimulate the production of procollagen, a protein that is good for your skin. Tomato paste has been shown to combat wrinkles and premature aging of the skin.

Turmeric

I love this multifaceted root. It helps with flu symptoms and aids in the healing of wounds and acne. It is a natural anti-inflammatory and detoxifies the liver. It helps rid the body of harmful substances, and is good for metabolism and digestion. It's a good remedy for heartburn, helps your body burn fat, and has a positive effect on bloating and cramping. Eating turmeric alongside black pepper helps your body maximize its absorption. I use it in my Feel-Good Drink (page 151).

Watercress

This green is a source of iodine and is rich in vitamin C. As a result, it's a good antioxidant and anti-inflammatory. Thanks to the sulfur-containing substances in watercress, it helps detoxify the liver, and is good for your skin, hair, and nails. It helps alleviate muscle and joint pain, reduces lactic acid buildup in muscles, and stimulates circulation. Super healthy!

Zucchini

Zucchini are rich in folic acid, potassium, magnesium, and vitamins A, B_1, and C. Due to their relatively high folic acid content, zucchini are the perfect food for women who are trying to conceive or who are already pregnant. They also aid in keeping your skin healthy your digestion system working, and supporting the nervous system.

Food as Medicine

Nobody is perfect. THERE ARE THOSE DAYS . . . YOU KNOW WHAT I'M TALKING ABOUT—*limp* HAIR, PASTY SKIN, UPSET *stomach*, AND LOW ENERGY. IT'S AT TIMES LIKE THESE THAT I HEAD TO MY *kitchen cupboards* TO LOOK FOR INGREDIENTS TO MAKE HEALTHY DISHES THAT CAN HELP RESOLVE *issues* LIKE THESE. THE *right* FOOD CAN OFTEN MAKE A BIG DIFFERENCE TO YOUR *well-being.* MY *Power Food recipes* ARE NOT ONLY TASTY, BUT MORE IMPORTANT, THEY ARE ALSO *healthy* AND GIVE YOU *energy.* PERFECT FOR A *happy and healthy life.*

Sleep

In short, sleeping is wonderful. Sleep deprivation can be pretty damaging. Seven to eight hours of sleep per night is optimal. Getting enough sleep improves your mood, your ability to concentrate, and your energy levels. It might be tough, but you really should do your best to get enough sleep.

POWER INGREDIENTS

Chamomile, chickpeas, magnesium, and sunflower seeds

POWER FOOD RECIPES

Drink my Feel-Good Drink (page 151) in the evening or eat something that contains lots of cacao powder—this is high in magnesium, which helps you relax and sleep. Try my Choco-Snack (page 83), for example, or Phyllon's Birthday Cake (page 119). Feel like something savory? Try my Chickpea Snack (see page 93), which is also high in magnesium.

Skin

You need to take care of your skin, both from the outside and from the inside. For healthy, glowing skin you need to drink enough water to keep your fluid balance in order. This means drinking 1½ to 2 quarts (1½ to 2 L) of water per day. Make sure you also eat healthy fats. If you suffer from problem skin, a juice made with sour fruits and green leafy vegetables will help.

POWER INGREDIENTS

Avocado, cucumber, fatty fish, green and orange vegetables, lemon, nuts, and plant oils

POWER FOOD RECIPES

Start the day with Popeye's Breakfast (page 27), as it contains lots of spinach. In the evening, try my Pasta with Salmon (page 70), as salmon is a nice fatty fish. Feel like something sweet? The Cheesecake (page 112) is full of nuts and lemon.

Hair

As long as it's a good hair day! Healthy hair isn't only a product of washing it with a good shampoo; you also need to care for it from the inside out. For shiny, strong hair you need to have adequate levels of vitamins A, B, and C, omega-3 fatty acids, and protein. Protein makes your hair more beautiful, so make sure you're eating enough of it. I also treat myself to a hair mask, consisting exclusively of coconut oil, which I leave on overnight. I rinse it out the next morning in the shower and my hair shines beautifully.

POWER INGREDIENTS

Black pepper, chia seeds, garlic, ginger, mushrooms, nuts, onions, pumpkin seeds, and tomatoes

POWER FOOD RECIPES

The protein in chia seeds makes your hair grow more quickly. My Chia-Banana Pudding (page 21) is the perfect power dish for you if your hair isn't growing well. The best choice for healthy hair is the Quinoa Salad (page 50), which is high in protein. My Red Juice (page 159) is also great for healthy hair because it is high in vitamins A and C.

Colds and Flu

When I have the flu, I try to get as much rest as possible. So I head to bed and sleep as much as I can. I consciously eat very little so that I give my body the time it needs to recover from the flu virus—it's so busy fighting the virus and removing waste products that there isn't much energy left to digest a heavy meal. That's why I focus on drinking lots of herbal tea and eating light meals like soups and salads when I'm ill. Vitamin C also provides my body with an energy boost.

POWER INGREDIENTS

Black pepper, bouillon, fruit, green leafy vegetables, onion, and seaweed

POWER FOOD RECIPES

My Feel-Good Drink (page 151) and my Detox Smoothie (page 146) are great choices when you're sick. Looking for a tasty but light evening meal? Try my Miso Soup (page 61) or Saoto Soup (page 54) with yellow sambal (page 142). These soups are very liquid and salty, which is exactly what you need when you're sweating a lot due to a fever. And the peppers in the sambal will help clear out your sinuses.

Gut

It is important to take care of your gut because it's the place where your body absorbs the nutrients you need to survive. You can do this by eating a healthy and varied diet that is low in sugar and high in fiber-rich fruits and vegetables. You also need to drink enough water—it's how you guarantee that your digestive system functions properly.

POWER INGREDIENTS

Bananas, chickpeas, dried fruit, flaxseeds, pumpkin, and water

POWER FOOD RECIPES

Fiber and fluid are essential to the proper functioning of your digestive system. My Crunchy Crackers (page 35) are full of seeds, which help produce bowel movements. Legumes like chickpeas are also high in fiber. The Homemade Hummus (page 128) is a healthy dip that will keep your digestive system strong. My Mean Green Smoothie (page 146) and the Rainbow Salad (page 36) contain lots of leafy greens that are high in chlorophyll, which helps cleanse the bowels. And above all, drink enough water! Drink a minimum of 1½ to 2 quarts (1½ to 2 L) of water and/or tea per day. Are you suffering from constipation? Drink even more!

Muscles and Bones

If you're active like I am, it's even more important that your diet includes the nutrients required for healthy muscles and bones. The demands on them are high! I get most of my calcium and protein from plant-based foods. The combination of calcium and magnesium is good for the maintenance of your bones, so make sure you get enough of both in your diet.

POWER INGREDIENTS

Chia seeds, dark green leafy vegetables, goat's milk products, nuts, samphire, seaweed, seeds, tahini, and whole-grain products like spelt

POWER FOOD RECIPES

A Kick-Start breakfast (page 17) is the perfect choice for athletes. The oats contain magnesium, calcium, and protein. A Hemp Smoothie (page 146) is also a good choice for breakfast because it's high in protein. In the evening, try my Casserole (page 75), which contains both healthy fats and protein.

Energy

Running, flying, stress, typing, talking, calling—like most of you, this is how I spend most days. And at around 4:00 in the afternoon, my energy levels tend to take a nosedive. To prevent this from happening, I try to make sure I relax often enough and get enough sleep. A good breakfast and healthy eating throughout the day (including snacks) help keep my energy levels up the whole day. And if that doesn't work, I just grab a cup of coffee like everyone else!

POWER INGREDIENTS

Avocado, bananas, berries, cayenne, fruit, lemon, and oatmeal

POWER FOOD RECIPES

My Primal Snack (page 92) is sweet and sour, which is tasty, and the berries and nuts it contains give me the energy I need. Around 4:00 in the afternoon, I will have a cup of my Hot Energy Drink (page 153). The combination of cayenne, honey, and vitamin C make it the perfect pick-me-up tea to counteract even the worst afternoon dip. And when I've really run out of gas, I'll make a Coffee Blast Smoothie (page 146). It's super tasty and is made with banana and coffee, a combo that gives me an instant energy boost.

I'm so thankful!

The biggest thank you goes to my *heit* and *mem*. You have taught me, motivated me, and inspired me to eat healthy. You've always done this with an open mind and without forcing the issue. Thanks to you, I've already been eating well and healthy my entire life. I know exactly what is good for my body and I can now do my work with conviction, love, and pleasure. I feel so unbelievably fortunate and I'm bursting with energy. Thank you for the inspiration and the amazing foundation you have given me!

To the most wonderful sister in the world! My big sister Doutzen has always been extremely supportive of me. *Skatsje*, you wish nothing but the best for me. I feel it and you also show it. You have always been there for me and I value that enormously. *Ik hâld fan dy!* And your beautiful son inspires me too. Dear Phyllon, I created many of my sweet recipes for you and because of you. Thank you for all of the fun, crazy, and love-filled moments we've shared.

During my time in New York, I found not only my love of healthy food, but also the love of my life. These past few years, my boyfriend Sid has thought along with me, seen me grow, and been my support and my port in a storm. Thank you, *chouchou*, for your critical perspective and your support of my development. Because of you, I'm more powerful in life. I love you!

Love, Rens!